This Roar Of Ours

This Roar Of Ours

To John ———
Hoping You Enjoy my Rants

JIM BOWMAN

To order additional copies of this book, contact:
Xlibris Corporation
1-888-795-4274
www.Xlibris.com
Orders@Xlibris.com
102671

*This book is thankfully dedicated to Carol,
without her support this book would still
reside in the windmills of my mind.*

Contents

Foreword

THE SUBJECT MATTER WITHIN THESE pages depicts our waywardness when we were dubbed "the silent majority." While this identity came into fashion long before my writing, a fair sampling from our "silent" period is the meat of this work.

First, I'd like to make clear that the following subject matter is not addressed from either a democrat or republican, liberal or conservative position. My approach is American.

What I mean by this is that for as long as I can remember, calling one's self an American has largely disappeared, and along the way, so has our national unity and pride. At some point, it occurred that what was taking place was the age old "divide and conquer" tactic. As time went on, this became quite obvious and, I might, say threatening.

There is little argument that the most divisive period in twentieth century America took place during "the sixties." As luck would have it, this was my generation's time in the bulwark. What followed was the "never would it be the same" rational. Ironically, from the most boisterous period came this most "silent" one. Whatever the reason, this "silent majority" began to form.

Although I am an old fashioned traditionalist, some even go so far as painting me with a Neanderthal brush, I cannot escape the fact that in most cases, what worked the best has been discarded. However, I fully realize that this happening is just part and parcel of our current dismay.

I remember the America before all this innovative reasoning took hold. I recall when the policeman was our friend, when Sunday was respected as the Sabbath and when proper attire and conduct was a classroom requirement. For this, I am extremely fortunate in that I can reference back through the prism of comparisons. Until now, this asset has been limited to a certain age.

It is this reference from which I've written my Op/ed pieces. As a traditionalist, I naturally revere our country's beginnings and thusly hold our founding documents on a high pedestal. In addition, I also recognize that the original intent of our founding fathers, when creating our Constitutional Republic, is the only avenue in which to understand and abide by their gifts of freedom and individual liberty. Hopefully, this message rings true within my writings.

As for my writings, they represent the outpouring from my frustrations at what I witnessed. I was fortunate in finding outlets for publishing during approximately the last twenty years. The topics are at random but remain pertinent as a comparative yardstick with today's Constitutional usurpations. I hope that readers will gain a more detailed perspective of today's events when referencing this look back. Especially so since our period for quiet submission has finally run its course.

I must point out that the POW/MIA issue obviously pre-dated this twenty year effort. All that it suggests makes this an ongoing and demanding topic. Indifferent to what the reader's age, this should remain "front and center" in all our hearts and minds. This is one question which America needs to resolve if she is to ever to be whole again.

I mentioned that our silence is finally over. This astounding, out of nowhere emergence of the Tea Party has already produced a different air in Washington. The best method for judging its worth is by assessing the means in which it is assailed. Since its message is unapproachable, the only available attack has been unfounded accusations and insults. Let this speak for itself.

Hopefully, my book will do the same. What follows is not often easy or comforting but maybe it will provoke some thought and action. In many regards, we have been lulled to sleep, often by subliminal nurturing into a certain perspective. This writing will challenge that slumber.

As my inspiration has been our founding era, what George Washington wrote in June, 1783 still applies. To quote, "At this auspicious period, the United States came into existence as a Nation, and if their Citizens should not be completely free and happy, the fault will be entirely their own."

Join me in returning America to its rightful place. JB

POW/MIA Report Not Surprising

(March 3, 1992)

THE AP RELEASE APPEARING IN the February 13th issue, of another POW/MIA photo being labeled as "bogus" comes as no surprise. Considering that over 1400 first-hand live sightings have met the same fate, photographic evidence will not be enough. I believe that what our government considered as "acceptable losses" has turned into an embarrassing issue which cannot be admitted. At this point, nothing short of a live walking and talking POW or an MIA will do.

This latest declaration is a complete reversal to a more detailed article that appeared in the December, 1991 issue of Soldier of Fortune magazine.

A thorough investigation was conducted by Dr. Michael Charney, whose field of expertise is forensic anthropology, along with fifty years of experience. He is also an internationally recognized expert in the field of human identification.

Dr. Charney compared facial dimensions from a 1961 wedding photo of Special Forces Captain Donald Carr to the "bogus" 1990 picture. After the two pictures were super imposed on 33 mm slides and projected by zoom lens to the same magnification, measurements of facial features were taken and found to match. Even "the ears were studied in detail as to the similarity of lobes, helix, concha and tragus. They matched."

At this stage of Dr. Charney's investigation, he turned to an authority in a different field for further collaboration and proof, a Dr. Patrick Fitzhorn, Department of Mechanical Engineering, Colorado State University.

Computer technology was employed in drawing the facial outlines in both pictures to 1/100 of an inch. Each outline had its distinguishing color for identification purposes. Superimposing the two outlines proved

11

that both pictures were of the same man. Also, Dr. Fitzhorn added, "the muscular structure of the face where he smiles is exactly the same."

Armed with this past essay, one can imagine why my frustrations led to this article. Also, as a Vietnam veteran, I personally believe that many Americans remained, against their will, in South East Asia at the time of our official departure.

Just the sheer number of sightings, that over the years have been reported, should suggest a very possible foundation of fact. I find it hard to believe, and increasingly insulting, that all such reports lead to dead ends or are actually "bogus!"

Following this line of thought, I further suspect that at this juncture, our government's consistent denial of POW/MIA's existence must continue in order to keep the possible truth from its citizens. Certainly, over 1400 first hand live sighting reports would go far in substantiating this uncomfortable belief.

Currently, our government is proceeding on a course that would call an end to the economic embargo and normalize relations with Vietnam. This of course, is being supported amid hopes of all the economic opportunities which it will no doubt entail.

The term "acceptable loss" is a military concept dealing with a predetermined number of casualties that the higher command is willing to accept in order to achieve a military objective. I suggest that since this original number has dwindled over the years, our losses have become more acceptable.

Reader's Mad At MADD

(January 2, 1994)

THE NOVEMBER 24ᵀᴴ ISSUE DETAILED MADD's uproar, in responce to official reports disclosing that the number of "drunken driving offenders" in 1992 is down twelve percent from the previous year. This brings their main purpose into sharper focus. This group sees it as a numbers game that is specifically geared towards prosecution. They hold little regard for preventive methods.

I thought that this reduction of drunken driving citations was what this organization was originally all about. I mean, one would think that their efforts are finally being rewarded. However, it's almost as though MADD would prefer drivers to be under the influence so that arrest numbers would validate their organizational importance.

MADD's obvious lack of interest towards the illegal detection methods which are now employed, the increased in public awareness and responsibility, and, most significantly, the indications that illustrate the positive direction road safety is taking, all combine to question this organization's true agenda and overall purpose.

Through this recent public disclosure, MADD fully expects politicians and law enforcement to begin a mad dash for making 1994 a record year for arrests. Further limitations and public restrictions will no doubt come into play.

Through it all, there is one very important statistic absent from MADD's public tirade. It seems that traffic deaths connected with alcohol have been reduced by twenty percent over the last two year period. Despite the supportive nature between these two statistics, MADD's only concern remains centered in the area of arrests, not in lives saved. It seems odd that this group, which was formed out of experiencing personal loss, would not

13

be rejoicing about the many lives saved by their insistent message. If safety takes a back seat when compared to proper arrest quotas, then I believe that MADD's credibility should come into question.

Recently, through a former relationship with a very highly placed public servant in the Pennsylvania legislature, my suspicions of political cowering under the MADD pressure was re-enforced. Agreeing to an "off the record" condition, my suspicions were substantiated as it was conveyed that politicians consider any voiced opposition to MADD as an act of political suicide. How sad to come face to face with the tail wagging the dog!

Fortunately, I'm not a politician so I'll rely on my freedom of speech for honest reflection. Any group or association that endorses a violation to our Constitution in order to further its own particular agenda qualifies, in my estimation, as being "un-American." The program which MADD is featuring is an increasingly glaring example of such an unworthy title.

In MADD's case, from their beginnings, they endorsed the system of "roadblocks." This, in fact, directly violates both the Federal and Pennsylvania Constitutions. While our Nation's Fourth Amendment expressly forbids this type of enforcement procedures, Article I, Section 8 of the Pennsylvania Constitution is also specific as to first establishing "probable cause" prior to actions against a citizen.

Whether at a State or Federal level, authority is limited through our Constitutional system. It is the "law of the land" and in this instance, also, the law of Pennsylvania. Citizens conform to laws. So must governments and their enforcement agencies.

While offenders are still apprehended by the suspect providing "probable cause," which draws the attention of law enforcement, the main weapon amassing higher arrest numbers is this un-Constitutional system of roadblocks. Contrary to the "presumption of innocence" which every citizen owns when appearing in court, the reverse is true when roadblocks are in operation. When stopped without any "probable cause," many drivers must prove their innocence.

In my mind, clearly, what began as a "good intentioned" effort by a few angry mothers wanting safer highways has morphed into a powerful lobby driven organization that endorses anti-Constitutional legislation. Their present agenda justifies this perspective.

Consider the preference for employing roadblocks. Essentially, they are in place to detect a degree of "guilt" that otherwise would often remain undetectable. The offense has been re-defined from "drunken driving," which usually provides clear guilt, to that of "under the influence," which requires such illegal detection methods.

The question to address, is whether MADD's target is the dangerous "drunken driver" or the often undetectable "under the influence" one?

Please do not get the impression that I support drunken driving or any irresponsible actions from behind the wheel. I do not! As a parent who thankfully has the child rearing years in his rear view mirror, I fully realize the potential dangers that drunken drivers, along with the assortment of other highway mishaps present. However, the integrity of our State and Federal laws must be maintained for ensuring societal order and respect.

Of equal danger are the groups, no matter how well intentioned, who amass a degree of influence so large that they influence and/or intimidate the passage of laws which are direct violations of our Constitution. I also find it discomforting that these same groups take it upon their own to set requirements for proper and efficient police enforcement.

And lastly, I find it highly offensive that representatives from this authoritative MADD assemblage find it necessary to follow a DUI suspect into the courtroom so that a proper sentencing will be assured.

Our society, and the enforcement of its laws, worked just fine before this demanding presence. And it will work just fine after our citizens realize that they themselves can best insure their own safety.

POW/MIA Issue 'Sinful'

(February 13, 1994)

AMID ALL THE DIVERSE PROBLEMS and issues which plague our country, this unanswered POW/MIA question deserves our nation's highest priority. We, as a people, owe this accounting, to our country and to the many families that have endured the pain and anguish associated with over twenty years of unproductive and/or inactive attention. I personally know of one local family (located in Delaware County, Penna.) who has waited for answers since 1965! For too long, this issue has been viewed as an embarrassment by those in our government. At this point, a sinful aura creeps over this long awaited and overdue accounting.

As a private citizen who personally believes that its long since been proven that Vietnam did knowingly hold American POWs after 1973 and continue to do so, the present day excavations around twenty and thirty year old crash sites seems a bit self defeating at best. After all these years, is this the most productive method of investigation? Strange, especially when one considers all the high-tech surveillance equipment available today, along with all the untold capabilities from maintaining our extensive and expensive intelligence community.

In order to make a fair judgment as to the degree of futility associated with this issue, a comparison should be made to another challenging question from our country's past. Consider in terms of time elapsed, the development of the first Atomic bomb must have been a snap!

From this comparative view, can one question that a twenty year effort stretches the limits of an honest effort? There very well could be a factor or unknown reason that's been consistent throughout this lengthy period which hinders any possibility for a successful conclusion.

I believed that this factor emerged in 1979 but was quickly smeared and disguised by an attempt to keep the lid upon this entire issue.

Briefly, the sometimes mentioned mindset to debunk or discredit is the culprit. Any investigator or investigation that attempts to disprove, discredit, or dismiss informational leads rather than honestly and thoroughly investigating such data is doomed to failure. A quick check into the results of a half-hearted twenty year search for POWs and MIAs tends to confirm this lackadaisical policy along with its inevitable lack of results.

Vietnam was proven to be untruthful as to an accurate accounting of our POWs when, in 1979, Marine PFC. Robert Garwood ingeniously forced his own release. This was the one and only time that our government, through their own documented actions, revealed so clearly their true intentions.

Although his return represented a possible wealth of information, our government's immediate response was its successful policy to discredit him personally, which also tended to nullify any information which he possessed. This treatment of PFC. Garwood is fact which cannot be denied and in itself offers a glimpse into the true conduct and methods that our government has employed over the past two decades.

Upon arriving in Bangkok from Vietnam, PFC. Garwood was read his rights, offered legal counsel, and placed under Marine guard. Back in the United States, our efficient government had already initiated court martial proceedings against him. Certainly a strange priority taken against the only POW to have come home from Vietnam after Vietnam supposedly released all they had in captivity in 1973. This should have been the last order of business from a government that was supposedly so dedicated to this issue being finally resolved.

Briefly, PFC. Garwood was found guilty of aiding and abetting with the enemy and of slapping a fellow POW. This guilty verdict essentially opened the door to continually discrediting PFC. Garwood in any and all printed articles that mentioned his name.

As became the practice, his name is almost always followed by, "who was found guilty of collaborating with the enemy," or even the untrue, "a defector during the Vietnam War." This second and false description can be found in the final report of the pretentious Senate Select Committee on POW/MIA Affairs.

In viewing the urgency of his court martial compared to the logical need to debrief PFC. Garwood, it is interesting to note that many former POWs were puzzled since they stated that Garwood's actions were no better or no worse than other POWs who were not prosecuted. Just as interesting were the comments made by the presiding judge at Garwood's court martial. His personal impression was, and I quote, "a travesty of justice."

A third governmental charge of desertion was quickly dropped due to the testimony of a fellow Marine who validated the circumstances which led to Garwood's capture. Supposedly, this false charge stemmed from a "no stone left unturned" type of investigation. This also attests to the degree or the limits to which the government would travel in order to discredit PFC. Garwood. Had it been proven, he would have been labeled a traitor forever.

To further illustrate the curious action of our government against a marine who normally would have been hailed an ingenuous hero, it is essential to understand what the Geneva Convention defines as the status of a POW. In a shorten version, it states that once a soldier is captured by the enemy, his status as a POW cannot be changed since his ability to make a free choice is taken away.

Also for consideration, as the war in Vietnam grew, our Pentagon examined the question of POW status. Mainly from our experience in the Korean War and fully realizing North Vietnam's un-acceptance of the Geneva Convention, the Pentagon agreed to a policy which essentially stated that any soldier who wanted to be considered a deserter had to do so at the time he deserted. A desertion charge could not be applied after a period of capture. No wonder the presiding judge left the proceedings with his pro-Garwood impression.

As anyone can quickly recognize, these actions against PFC. Garwood show a consistency to debunk, discredit and dismiss. They certainly aren't consistent with an honest and truthful effort to gain the long awaited information regarding this heartbreaking travesty.

One other embarrassing fact stands out in this PFC. Garwood case. It only took our government eight years to begin the debriefing process.

I wrote this not as a Vietnam veteran but as a father of a twenty-one year old son. Our government's responsibility concerning all our POWs, MIAs, and KIAs is paramount.

I am fully aware of the hardships and sacrifice asked of our military personal. I am also sadly aware of the hardships and sacrifices of those who wait at home. The only exception I have is that in either case, it shouldn't require over twenty years to reach closure.

Action Insulted All Veterans

(March 20, 1994)

THE RECENT LIFTING OF THE economic embargo against Vietnam not only insulted veterans of all wars, it was particularly degrading to our national integrity since there are too many unanswered questions concerning our POW/MIAs. The President's speech in which he announced the lifting only heightened this disrespect. I suppose his former pledge that the embargo would remain in place until we receive the "fullest possible accounting" ended up in the same circular file as did his other campaign promises.

Prior to the official ending of this embargo, Clinton also revealed his impression concerning the gullibility of the American public when he stated that his decision would not be based on "commercial interests." In order for us to believe this, as Clinton apparently thinks we will, he must consider us akin to mushrooms which are kept in the dark and fed that gooey stuff.

His fairy tale approach to commencing business with a communist government was highlighted by his White House spokeswoman, Dee Dee Myers, when she uttered the ding dong statement, "We'll be able to make more progress once we expand our relationship with Vietnam."

Since this was in reference to the POW/MIA issue, what does she expect will happen or be discovered by civilian businessmen and woman? Maybe she believes that these three piece suits will devote their lunch hour to searching the jungles and mountains for our lost personnel.

Many may view Clinton as unlucky or unfortunate in that he inherited an issue that many predecessors ignored. I disagree.

On a level that mushrooms can understand, if a married couple buys a house with the full realization that the basement has a history of leaking during rainy periods, then they accept that problem. Likewise, Clinton was well aware of the "leaks" that came with the office. My problem with the President is that after he acquired this "house," the leaks went unattended and now he's trying to sell it as a property with an indoor pool.

In his speech, Clinton stated, "Today our nation is one in honoring those who served and pressing for answers about all those who did not return. This decision today, I believe, renews that commitment and our constant, constant effort never to forget . . . until our job is done."

Personally, I doubt this man knows the true meaning of the word "honor," especially when used in connection with the Vietnam war. After all, this is a person who had to be coached on how to execute a military salute—and I might add, unsuccessfully.

Now I have thought of a speech that Clinton could have used, which probably would have been closer to the truth. Wouldn't it have been refreshing to turn on the TV and hear our President say, "Listen people, the embargo is in shreds since many of the participating nations have already defected and are doing business with the Communists. Our nation might not be 'one' with my decision, but I have decided today that in order to offset the disastrous economic effects which NAFTA will surely produce, our greedy business community can join in the stampede. This might not be the most honorable course of action since we really haven't tried to settle the POW/MIA question as of yet, but business is business and our economic base is in shambles."

Putting Clinton's recent announcement aside, I must point out that he is a newcomer to this charade of cover-up and deception. The players in this shameful act not only include all former Presidents since 1973, but also a vast majority of Congress who have declined to voice opposition or even question this and other shameful and immoral policies.

Out of all the players, naturally the ones who have garnered the limelight stand out as most responsible. Oddly enough, the three who come to mind happen to be Vietnam veterans with impressive war records. Just as their decorations represent their degree of duty during the war, their public statements and conduct in connection with the Senatorial Investigation into the POW/MIA issue now raise questions as to their current true intentions.

To a man, they supported the lifting of the embargo long before it became fact and in roughly the last year, have had nothing but praise for the amount of assistance the government of Vietnam has provided. However, they all failed to mention that our country paid millions for Vietnam's increased efforts.

Prior to the Senatorial Investigation, our government conducted an investigation into the overall policy that our country has manifested in accounting for its POW/MIAs at the conclusion of past hostilities with all Communist regimes. It was uncovered that our country's policy has remained the same since World War I, and that this course of action, or non-action, could be viewed as criminal.

Our POW/MIA policy is best described in a letter written by Sen. Jesse Helms on May 23, 1991 that states, "Despite public announcements to the contrary, the real internal policy of the U.S. Government was to act upon the presumption that all MIAs were dead." He further states, "any evidence that suggest that a MIA might be alive was uniformly and arbitrarily rejected." In addition, Sen. Helms writes, "our government downplayed or denied the reports of POW/MIAs, and failed to take adequate steps to prove or disprove the reports, while elements in our government pursued policies intended to make diplomatic recognition and financial support of the revolutionary regimes possible."

This last quote is germane to the present day lifting of the embargo but equally important, those quotes of Sen. Helms, from the findings of his investigation, not only substantiates the existence of the current denial policy but dates its age at three quarters of a century.

One would think that armed with this summation of such a shameful policy, the following Senate Investigation would soon uncover the truth. Especially when Sen. John Kerry—a highly decorated Vietnam veteran—was its Chairman.

When considering the alarming findings which Sen. Helms revealed, verses the declaration from Sen. Kerry, along with the absence of any concrete results from the investigation, I find it incredulous to first officially end this investigation and then to lift the embargo.

Many separate investigations stemming from isolated reports and information provide hints of at least a lackadaisical effort of investigating.

Consider the shock and power to his words when the President of Russia stated that Vietnam sent American POWs to his country. Despite denials from the Vietnamese government, this was incriminating testimony that those honest and helpful Vietnamese weren't as they appeared. Our government considered President Yeltsin to have "misspoke." Diplomacy took a back seat by this denial.

In April 1993, a top secret document was discovered in the Russian archives which was written by a "senior North Vietnamese General" which raised the official number of POWs that Vietnam held from 368 to 1205. Of course, within ten days, this was found to be false by an investigator who said the document was "authentic but simply inaccurate." The Vietnamese themselves helped to clear up this question when they said the document was based on "bad intelligence."

Then we have the case of whether there was an underground detention facility built under Ho Chi Minh's tomb which was used to hold American POWs. This was a classic example of why this charade ended with little or no results.

Into the Senate hearings charged the DIA (Defense Intelligence Agency) with their findings. Now it should be noted that this agency is charged with the overall investigation of all POW/MIA information. They quickly denied (surprise) the possibility of such an underground facility since "the water table in the Vietnamese capitol is too high."

This sounded impressive and its basic premise was such that to think otherwise was foolhardy. Again, this received national headlines which led the public to believe that this attempt was, at best, a grabbing at straws idea.

However, what was not reported with the same amount of coverage, if it was reported at all, was that another agency, the DNA (Defense Nuclear Agency), was called in to conduct a second investigation into this matter. Their findings were quite the opposite of the DIA's. Not only did the DNA confirm the existence of the underground facility, they provided some of the structural dimensions as well.

I mention these instances only to substantiate my amazement at our three Vietnam veteran Senators, Kerry, Kerrey and McCain. Their consistent questioning and doubting attitudes during the investigations, coupled with their repeated praise of Vietnamese efforts suggest that there was a second agenda addressed.

I suppose that some will view my thoughts as "crying over split milk," or that of being a crazy Vietnam veteran who "can't let go of the war." I call it setting the record straight! Although our political leaders wouldn't recognize anything that resembles a record straightening, I believe most others will.

I guess what I'm trying to say is that we may be considered mushrooms, but don't expect us to say that the gooey stuff that we are fed tastes good!

DUI Legislation 'Inequitable'

(August 14, 1994)

ANY AMENDMENTS TO A PRESENT law that is based outside the legal boundaries of our Constitution can only continue down the same illegal path. Two pieces of legislation that will shortly be included to our present DUI law surely validates this statement. Appropriately, all support for such anti-American measures deserves the distended outrage of all law abiding and tax paying citizens. This is especially true when support for such practices can be found among those we elect.

Both these proposals are Federally instigated and supported through large monetary incentives which dilutes the importance of Constitutional rights and erases the ability of individual State governments to operate independently.

When considering that in the oath of office, all elected officials swear to "preserve, protect and defend" the Constitution, the passage of such measures should reflect a basic disobedience and/or dereliction of the public's trust.

The first proposed addition would further cripple our State's largest employing industry, the tavern and restaurant segment of our economy. The lowering of the BAC (Blood Alcohol Content) from .1 to .08 will effectively tighten the strangle-hold that presently restricts income and additional hiring of these privately owned establishments. In spite of this well known fact, Pa. Rep. Matt Ryan comments on the proposed lowering, "if enacted, will also result in the receipt of $3 million to $4 million in additional Federal Highway Safety money." This type of justification is not only intrusive and abusive to State authority, the question of the law's legitimacy becomes victimized, as does all other possible ramifications when Washington throws its wallet around, or so it seems.

23

Contrary to all the original medical data and law enforcement concerns, which were minutely studied prior to enacting the BAC level of .1, there now suddenly arises a need to reduce what was first accepted to be a fair and workable BAC level. Again, in the words of Rep. Ryan, "some research indicates impairment starts as low as .015 per cent. According to the National Safety Council, impairment for most individuals occurs at .05 per cent and that all drivers have their driving performance significantly impaired at .08 per cent."

One stumbling block remains. Where was all this information for determining "impairment" when the original .1 BAC was mutually accepted and was determined to be just and effective by both the medical and law enforcement experts? By Rep. Ryan's review, this may represent just an intermediary step before another BAC adjustment takes place.

This suggests that the State of Pennsylvania has re-interpreted the law's original intent from one of combating the menace of drunken driving to that of determining the fine line of alcohol influence.

Trying to keep this DUI legislation in its proper perspective, mention must be made as to the high-handed enforcement methods which were incorporated into the DUI legislation from day one. When one reads the Pennsylvania Constitution, the injustice associated with the implementation of roadblock enforcement is immediately recognized. Similar to our Federal Constitution, Pennsylvanians are Constitutionally protected from unreasonable searches and seizures without first establishing "probable cause."

Isn't it ironic that a group which is considered by many to operate outside the law—the Hell's Angels—care enough about their Constitutional freedoms to take the New Jersey State Police to court because of indiscriminate stoppings without "probable cause?"

Public apathy, which surfaces especially around election time, has given the politician the impression that they can enact any legislation without fear of voter reprisal. The second pending DUI add-on is a clear indication of this insulting mindset.

The ALS (Administrative License Suspension) proposal is a fancy term that essentially administers punishment prior to a court appearance. This Constitutional violation may also become law shortly.

Unknown by most Pennsylvania citizens, PennDOT helped draft this ALS legislation and will be assigned the task of conducting preliminary hearings at which time the suspect will have the opportunity of regaining his or her license until the official court date and subsequent ruling is determined. PennDOT will presently charge a $100 fee to support the cost of each hearing. The imbecilic feature of this PennDOT fee is that it's already acknowledged to be insufficient and will certainly require increases once this charade is enacted.

One glaring aspect with these PennDOT hearings is that although the "suspect" could eventually be exonerated from the DUI charge, this preliminary hearing will remain in the individual's record. Clearly, PennDOT's importance and involvement will blossom in the future.

Some logic and concern was voiced by Rep. Thomas M. Tigue, when he stated, "PennDOT should not be in the judicial business and the police officers should not be the jury." Constitutionally, this is correct!

The reason or cause for the ALS proposal would be comical if it weren't such a serious injustice. It seems that the State capital is awash with "procedural delays and backlogs," associated with processing the DUI onslaught. This government slowdown has resulted in an average eleven month delay before a suspect appears in court. According to the rantings of organizations such as MADD, this period affords ample time for the suspect to again drive drunk. This reasoning sounds to me like the "suspect" has already been found guilty.

In other words, after enacting a DUI law that our State was essentially ill-prepared to effectively process, they now deem it necessary to further restrict the rights of its citizens. Harrisburg's proposed attempt to shift the blame and the solution onto the public demonstrates their inability to face the reality of its own shortcomings.

A sampling of statements by supporters of such anti-Constitutional measures exemplifies the freedom crunching direction that Harrisburg has and will continue to follow.

Beginning with Cheryl Hull, State Executive Director of MADD, referring to the ALS proposal, "with the immediacy of the suspension, people will know its no game anymore." This statement is a clear example of the delusion brought about by a sense of superiority and power.

Then we have the confusing reaction from Rebecca Brown, President of MADD, when confronted with the declining number of traffic arrests involving alcohol. Instead of the euphoria, which should have had Ms. Brown beaming with a pride from accomplishment, she surprisingly remarked, "enforcement has faltered." Ms. Brown's audacity went so far as to evaluate State Police efforts throughout the Nation at the "B-minus" level.

Someone should inform Ms. Brown that since DUI records have been kept, arrests have consistently diminished and that a parallel statistic revealed that "alcohol-related traffic deaths declined twenty per cent from 1990 to 1992. Also tell Ms. Brown that Department of Transportation officials admit that this represents "the largest two year drop ever recorded."

However, the statements from Ms. Brown and Ms. Hull are mild in comparison to those of Steven L. Schmidt, Executive Director of the Pennsylvania DUI Association. His fascist mindset rears its ugly head when he stated, "we need to weigh out the interest of the State, highway safety, and the carnage that is occurring with the individual's rights."

In conclusion, the inequities of the entire DUI legislation can be appreciated almost daily in the media. More often than not, suspected offenders are labeled with the term "drunken driver" when in reality of the law's own designation, the crime is "under the influence."

The present consideration of lowering the BAC level will only increase the enforcement efforts toward the fine line of alcohol influence while the media and groups such as MADD continue to count the totals under the column labeled "drunken driving." Such false reporting should be anticipated with the illegal enforcement of a changing offense.

Smoky Super Bowl

(February 12, 1995)

THE HYPOCRISY, WHICH HAS BECOME so common place in today's society, was never as evident as it was during the recent Super Bowl broadcast. The pre-game and half-time celebrations, along with an expensive TV advertisement, brought home this point with rare clarity This was accomplished with a total disrespect to both the ticket buying fans and the many million viewers at home.

Not intending to be completely negative, the highlight of the Super Bowl coverage was Mrs. Gifford's rendition of our National Anthem. In recent memory, seldom have our citizens been treated to such a genuinely respectful and heartfelt rendition. Clearly, the viewing audience of the world, and especially those in attendance, had to take notice.

However, it is incredulous that over seventy thousand unsuspecting fans purchased tickets to what they thought would be a football game rather than two attempts to see how much smoke Robbie Stadium could hold. The smoke filled pre-game show was duplicated by the equally smoky halftime festivities.

In respect to our national anti-smoking crusade's emphasis regarding the question of "secondary smoke" and its associated health issues, it would appear that the degree to which the smoke encompassed the stadium had to be somewhat intrusive and obviously hypocritical. It is inconceivable how city ordinances could be in compliance or how the associated permits could be issued for such an intense display of what had to be a chemically based "exhale" resulting in a fog density similar to San Francisco.

One can only imagine the thoughts that Gov. Lawton Childes must have pondered while watching these festivities. Isn't he the same Florida

Governor who boasted that his State will "take the Marlboro Man to court?"

It's apparent that the city of Miami assigns little credence to Childs' anti-tobacco grandstanding and definitely hasn't followed along with the draconian measures recently taken by the city of New York. The "Big Apple" has a ban on smoking in certain outdoor settings, which would certainly have nullified permission for those Super Bowl celebrations.

This objection might seem picayune to some but smoke is smoke. Many outdoor stadiums have instituted smoking regulations against fans who would indulge. Somebody better tell the powers to be that you can't have it both ways. The high density of smoke engulfing Robbie Stadium reduced the individual's secondary smoke to a mere trifle. Also, how does one in attendance even view the performance if he or she is unable to see the field? Just a thought, one which was probably swept under the advertising rug.

What stood out was the lack of an exodus from the thousands of non-smokers who were in attendance. Could we imagine these same individuals walking into a restaurant with a comparable amount of dense smoke? I think not.

To compound this hypocrisy, fans at home were treated to their own version of insults. One of the advertisements featured in the pricy Super Bowl time slots foretold of a new TV program with the come on of "sex, drugs and murder." The only thing missing was "rock and roll."

In a society which supposedly is so concerned over the moral and ethical decay confronting our young, this glowing example of "money talks" slams home the message of just how major corporations view their responsibilities. This insult became unduly emphasized when considering the game's early evening viewing. The Super Bowl was always assumed to be decent and proper viewing for the young.

As a football fan old enough to remember a time when players played because they loved the game, and half time festivities composed of marching bands and majorettes, why has the slick promoters and advertisers chosen to devalue those traditional and often patriotic half-time celebrations? Is thirty minutes per year too much devotion to our values? And is this overkill style of "entertainment" in harmony with the nature of the game's honest and hard won struggle?

In the wake of football's biggest day, how many hours will pass before our nation's media returns to their repetitive messages warning the public against the evils of smoking or of the need for parents to "police" the TV programs which their children may view?

There is a bottom line to what took place at Super Bowl XXIX. All the FDA and EPA reports "don't wash" if you were one of the seventy thousand who were asphyxiated in Miami.

Totalitarianism

(September 29, 1995)

THE LABELING OF RANDY WEAVER as a "white separatist" seems to produce a response in many Americans that almost condones the murderous actions by government authorities at Ruby Ridge. In contrast, if we are to remain a free society, this apathetic posturing coupled with false assurances which tend to insulate us from such brutal reality must stop. The notion that best reflects this attitude, "that doesn't pertain to me, that's only directed at those people," represents a feeding ground for totalitarianism. At some point, Americans must realize that we all could be "those people."

Somewhere along the line, our government has been transformed from one that operated with integrity and humanity to one that is becoming increasingly unaccountable for its actions.

The normality of our government hinges upon a delicate balancing act of its limited authority, in order to maintain an orderly and peaceful society through its benevolent care and protection. This calm order is rendered to the people through a system of laws which call for legal enforcement through a fair and impartial court proceeding, which culminates with a just punishment for the crime committed.

Today, the enforcement element to this balancing act has been degraded into a brutish and abusive power which may produce swift and lethal results.

In the aftermath of Ruby ridge, a Congressional investigative team is presently conducting hearings to determine just what led up to the confrontation and to determine the possible culpability of those who participated.

The associated agencies involved included the FBI, the BATF and the U.S. Marshall service. All have joined forces for a defense of their actions and in doing so, have heightened the growing fears of many Americans.

In judgement of the Government's actions on August 21 and 22, 1992, it should be understood that Mr. Weaver was accused, not convicted of a crime. For whatever reason, he failed to appear for a specific court date.

This would hardly qualify as a justifiable crime for the government's subsequent actions which Mr. Potts, who was the FBI official in charge at Ruby Ridge, deemed necessary.

Mr. Potts described the event as "the most dangerous situation into which the FBI had ever gone." This perception was the major reason for changing "the rules of engagement" from one of basic self defense to the unconstitutional premise of shooting to kill any armed male adult. Even with this broad and expanded authorization, the deaths of Vicki Weaver and her fourteen year old son, could hardly qualify as armed male adults. Mr. Potts' revised approach, combined with its lethal results, should appropriately be termed, "overkill."

It has been reported that Randy Weaver's fourteen year old son was killed in a "shootout" with Federal authorities. The term "shootout" would seem to imply a face to face confrontation. His son was shot in the back!

The most ludicrous of defense statements, which was first uttered at a previous inquiry as the sniper in question has since "taken the Fifth," pertained to the head shot that caused the death of Vicki Weaver. It seems that his target was a man fleeing into the cabin and that Mrs. Weaver death was actually a mistake. What's that mean, it didn't count?

In our society, whether it be the response from an individual citizen or from the local or Federal levels of law enforcement, there can be no justification for shooting a person who is running away and who in doing so, does not present a threat.

The overall message associated with any support of the Government's Ruby Ridge action introduces a mentality of lawlessness by any agency supporting this abuse of deadly power. The only appropriate outcome to this Congressional investigation is the immediate filing of the necessary criminal charges against all those responsible.

The sad legacy of Ruby Ridge is that it provided the blueprint that would encompass the additional use of military tanks, against American citizens at Waco.

The Concept Of Probable Cause

(June 9, 1996)

WHAT GAVE CLINTON, DOLE AND Gingrich the authority to publicly criticize a federal judge in New York for his decision to dismiss evidence that was obtained from an illegal vehicle stop? The judge ruled that the stop was not based upon "probable cause" and as such, the resulting evidence was inadmissible. This federal interference is a direct violation of the State's rights found within our Constitution. The fact that the judge finally reversed his ruling only compounds the magnitude of federal meddling.

The media coverage included Clinton's threat to "ask the judge to quit," Dole suggesting that the judge should face impeachment and Gingrich blaming the judicial decision as a "perfect reason why we are losing our civilization." What individual judge could withstand such a verbal lashing?

This bi-partisan action reveals a Washington tendency that disregards any legitimacy associated with our Constitution and promotes this type of abusive action all the way down the ladder of authority.

Unfortunately, persuading the judge to change his decision has irreversibly opened the door of doubt and criticism in all future judgments dealing with the issue of "probable cause," not to mention committing a personal attack upon the integrity of the judge in question.

Vital to this development is the precarious position of our nation's Fourth Amendment. For over the last twenty years, our top legal beagles on the Supreme Court have issued interpretations and add-ons that undermines the amendment's original intent.

This amendment states in part, "the right of the people to be secure in their persons, houses, papers and effects, against unreasonable searches and seizures, shall not be violated, and no warrants shall issue, but upon probable cause, supported by oath or affirmation."

As anyone can readily see, the essential element of "probable cause" must first be established, prior to taking action against an individual citizen. In the last twenty years, this requirement has steadily been under attack.

In 1974, our Supreme Court authorized the concept of "warrantless searches." This ruling can be based upon receiving permission from "a third party who possesses common authority or sufficient relationship to the premises."

Again, in 1984, in the case entitled "United States v. Leon," the Supreme Court established a "good faith" add-on that defended a search warrant that was issued without "probable cause." The legal reasoning recognized that since authorities didn't realize that the warrant was defective, they operated in "good faith." The search and ensuing evidence was admissible.

To make matters worse, back in February, 1995, our Federal government passed legislation in the House, HR 666, which further cements the future demise of our Fourth Amendment. This legislation permits evidence that is obtained without a search warrant if police acted with an "objectively reasonable belief" and observed the Constitutional protections against unreasonable search and seizures.

At some point, it must become obvious that there is a clear intent to reduce our citizen's Fourth Amendment rights.

This recent legislation, HR 666, is an asinine example of just how confused the amendment is becoming. How can a police officer exert "good faith" or be guided by an "objectively reasonable belief" and still remain true to Fourth Amendment mandates? Especially if they are without a search warrant that must be based on "probable cause!"

It could very easily be argued that "probable cause" disappeared with the advent of DUI roadblocks. Through an issue that society found deploring, "probable cause" became a needless precaution.

By using a ludicrous analogy, which is only meant to reveal the endless application of "good faith," maybe the offender who is caught by such illegal fishnet methods should say, "Sir, I was unaware of being over the limit. I was just making a 'good faith' effort to get home." Such legislation may produce countless legal actions by both the authorities and the public.

In a very practical sense, police currently operate without the guidelines of "probable cause" on Friday, Saturday and Sunday nights, only to return to normal duties during the week which respects Fourth Amendment standards.

If only on a subconscious level, this Constitutional safeguard becomes viewed as an unnecessary obstacle that only hinders the apprehension of criminals.

Both the citizens and law enforcement agencies must decide whether it's preferable to live and operate under our Constitution or is it better to "play it by ear." The natural tendencies of government will always trade-off individual rights in order for it to grow larger and more powerful.

The balance of authority, with respect to individual rights, rests solely on the issue of "probable cause." To expeditiously discount its proven necessity, for the purpose of attaining easier arrest procedures, is not only superficial but will prove to be a dangerous door opening alternative.

The concept of "probable cause" must be respected by citizens, law enforcement officials and politicians such as Clinton, Dole and Gingrich. It provides the fairest of ground to initiate any criminal prosecution proceedings, especially against a citizen who is "presumed innocent until proven guilty!"

Americans Have Cause For Alarm

(October 20, 1996)

MANY WHO AUTOMATICALLY DISCOUNT THE "conspiracy theory" do so without any general knowledge or even curiosity. Considering what's at stake, this is a luxury our citizens can least afford. If only for the peace of mind that truth provides, we all owe it to ourselves, to make an attempt at understanding why a substantial segment of Americans believe so strongly in its existence.

Essential with this attempt is an understanding of the make-up or motives surrounding this theory. The media's term "wacko" has been selected for a purpose. It automatically eliminates any possible validity to the discussion based upon our own individual "wacko" images. Thusly, conversation is cut short just from mentioning the subject of a conspiracy. It's effective and it was meant to be.

Getting past this dead-end attitude, it should be interesting to note what causes curiosity in one individual while another remains unmoved. Money or fame does not come from espousing such a foreboding premise. It might very well be that an old fashioned love of country carries this message. Also, a true concern for their children's future adds urgency to their beliefs. There is also a value of self knowing that each in our own small way attempts to assure our present day freedoms and opportunities to future generations. This is not to belittle those who discount the theory as being un-American or not caring about the future. It's quite the opposite. It may just come down to one's personal habits determining our curiosity levels.

In a very practical sense, one doesn't readily embrace threats of insecurity or the idea that "something doesn't add up." However, this uneasiness may begin to ferment from a growing list of unexplained but factual events. Current policies add to this uncertainty.

How do we justify an American President that publicly anticipates the coming "world order?" What makes another American President blatantly defy his sworn oath of office while exhibiting his preference for loyalty to the dictums of the United Nation's Charter? Why has our government endorsed and encouraged the relocation of American corporations overseas? What legitimized the discounting of the public's supportive vote for California's Prop. 187?

Certainly, these facts and events represent dangers to our Country and our Constitution. On an individual basis, each lack a conspiratorial slant. When viewed together, along with an overview of our Country's policies since WWII, questions appear which are by their very nature intimidating.

In addition to these questionable policies comes the consistent parade of their failures. In judging just this element of consistent setbacks, one may conclude that the law of probabilities has been greatly stretched. Even the catch-all of "dumb luck" would produce a better performance.

Consider when America emerged from WWII, she was the most powerful and militarily successful country in the world. So, why this need for creating a foreign based United Nations organization? America certainly didn't need any assistance in defending her shores.

By joining the United Nations, America eventually relinquished its independent decision-making and protective capabilities by President Truman's conspicuous adherence to an international charter over our Constitution. The subsequent sacrifice in Korea and Vietnam attests to the overall UN authority overseeing both conflicts. While providing the bulk of manpower and financing, our effort was limited to the UN concept of containment and negotiated peace rather than America's goal for attaining victory.

During the intervening years between Korea and Vietnam, America revealed, in a most obvious but dishonorable fashion, just how impotent and subordinate it had become to the UN.

In 1956, in part due to the urgings of the American financed Voice of America, the Hungarians successfully revolted against Russian oppression. During their brief five days of freedom, they requested American assistance. Mainly, assistance in the form of U.S. diplomatic recognition for their newly established free country. They were proud of the fact that they accomplished this without U.S. intervention or military aid.

Instead of a simple acknowledgement of their efforts and success, not to mention their sacrifice, President Eisenhower, that gifted military leader who eliminated Nazi oppression from Europe, simply turned the entire matter over to the United Nations. The magnitude of our disgraceful reaction to the Hungarian Revolution cannot be, nor should it be, minimized nor discounted. Needless to say, Russia reacted to our official indifference by quickly re-invading the country with overpowering force and vengeance.

This American refusal to recognize Hungary, a country that fought and gained its freedom on its own, stands in stark contrast to our future efforts in Vietnam. Where was the consistency with the American policy to defend freedom? And why this drastic reversal such a short time later?

A sad revelation to our Hungarian disgrace surfaced four years later through the efforts of then Congressman Michael Feighan, D. Ohio. He released a State Department cablegram, sent to the Yugoslavian dictator, Tito, during Hungary's five days of freedom. Quoting from its contents, "The Government of the United States does not look with favor upon Governments unfriendly to the Soviet Union on the borders of the Soviet Union."

With this type of un-American policy in effect, I want to know who or what is controlling our Nation's foreign policies. Although the sad result in Hungary is but one instance of a national policy which blatantly refrains from promoting freedom, it points to a mindset within our Government that is actually responsible for our current conspiracy debate.

Unknown to the American public, and for very good reasons, there is an elitist organization that first attained power following WWII and has continued its growth to the present. The current Administration contains hundreds of its members in key Governmental positions. Its influence and power transcends both political parties since Bush and Clinton can be counted among its members.

To quickly sum up the goals of this group, way back in 1950, the international banker and member of this group, James P Warburg stated, "We shall have world government, whether or not we like it. The question is only whether world government will be achieved by consent or by conquest."

Certainly, with such a recorded statement, this should create a cause for alarm. The mindset represented in such a remark suggests an arrogance that is strengthened by the knowledge of developments not made public.

We have all heard of our recent Presidents talk of the coming new world order. When considering the age of Mr. Warburg's prediction, how close is it to reality?

While each of us must decide the validity of such a treasonous eventuality, maybe something Confucius said many years ago can help focus our scrutiny. That ancient wise man cautioned, "Look at the means which man employs; consider his motive, observe his pleasures. A man simply cannot conceal himself."

By the way, how many of us know the name of this secret American organization? That's because the first requirement with a successful conspiracy is secrecy.

Media Lacks Responsibility

(August 10, 1997)

MORE THAN EVER, OUR PRESENT day news industry acts in an unabashed fashion. This is a result from not being held accountable to the former high standards, which previously defined the journalism trade. For reasons that can only be assumed, it either discounts the former requirement for investigative reporting or it often follows the positions and policies of government, for the expressed purpose of instilling a particular public reaction or opinion. Neither of these current traits can co-exist with the expectation for the accuracy and truth which should characterize our society's free press.

Replacing journalism's essential needs are the gross errors and the selective omissions which presently permeates the trade. Examples are as plentiful as they are undeniable.

Its most recent example centered upon the media's attention detailing the proposed expansion of NATO by the inclusion of three former communist bloc countries. The reported figures that estimate the total cost for such an expansion exemplifies the extent of such irresponsible journalism.

Thirty-five billion dollars was the price tag which Clinton considered necessary in order to upgrade the three new countries to NATO standards. It was reported that this cost will be equally divided by America, Europe and the three new NATO members.

Grade school students can divide three into thirty-six. So can most journalists. It should be fairly easy to settle upon the approximate figure of slightly more than $11.5 billion as being the shared American price tag.

Now maybe my expectations of those in the news media are a bit exaggerated since Clinton's prediction of an annual $200 million bill extending over thirteen years went without any serious media questioning.

Again, basic multiplication of thirteen payments of $200 million comes to a meager $2.6 billion, roughly $9 billion short! A more realistic yearly figure for payment would lie somewhere around an annual $900 million mark. With such a great disparity, is it any wonder as to why the President would choose introducing the public to the lower figure? It remains puzzling as to why a follow-up report, correcting those estimates, never appeared in print or mention by the various TV news programming.

Going back to the early months of 1997, Clinton selected four new cabinet appointees. The press saturated the public with a series of newspaper articles that introduced the four to the American public. These presentations detailed both their professional accomplishments and provided a glance into their personal lives.

Missing, however, among all the detailed accounts of Madeleine Albright, Richard Cohen, Bill Richardson and Sandy Berger was their common tie of membership in the very secretive coalition of The Council on Foreign Relations, or more commonly, the CFR. This omission seems more than just a little odd when realizing that the President, who selected these individuals, is also a CFR member in good standing.

Hold your "conspiracy theory" laughter and pause to objectively consider this unreported association. Ask yourself, just how much is known about this secretive group. Then ask yourself as to why there are hundreds of like minded members employed at various federal levels in our government?

Also interesting to compare is the intense coverage of the recent trial of Timothy McVeigh verses the media's lack of interest and coverage with grand jury hearings that are currently taking place side by side. How many Americans have read or are familiar with Oklahoma Congressman Key? He was responsible for amassing well over 13,000 signatures for the expressed purpose of conducting a State investigation into a possible federal cover-up of the Oklahoma City bombing. One should automatically think that with such alarming implications, along with the support required for calling this official inquiry by those closest to the scene, that this would certainly deserve some degree of media attention.

A few years ago, the media reported that the two rounds of military base closings were for the expressed purpose of saving three billion dollars. What the press again failed to report was the mind-boggling results which deserved public attention. Not only did the base closings, along with the loss of civilian jobs, not save three billion, it actually cost taxpayers $143 million. This charge was in response to the vast environmental cleanup procedures which were required.

Presently, Clinton is proposing another similar round of closures and citing the same reason. These facts, if made available, would question why our President continues this policy which adds substantial costs to our annual budget. This lack of investigative reporting, and/or reporting all of the facts, permits a policy to go forward, which if presented in its totality, would possibly generate a different outcome.

Returning to this NATO expansion, has the reading public been kept abreast as to its need or the justification for such a large budget expense? NATO is a regional military alliance which falls under the auspices of the United Nations. On the other side of the world, a similar UN alliance known as SEATO didn't work out too well for our country.

Additionally, NATO was a cold war invention designed to offset possible Russian expansion. Today, the Berlin Wall is history and so is the Russian threat since the former USSR is now a participant in world trade and a peaceful member of our "global village." What drives this continuing need for NATO, let alone its expansion?

These are some of the points which will never be addressed by our illustrious press. The emphasis which our Forefathers placed on establishing a freedom of the press has been marginalized by the selective and slanted reporting that contains more filler than fiber. The American reader is now a victim of misinformation, omission and revision which helps shape certain outlooks and opinions.

Sixty years ago, Germans were fed a constant diet of governmental propaganda. We Americans still foolishly cherish our media as the basic right and information source for all our citizens. Contrasting our system of justice with that of today's media output, the former is in place to deter the individual from abusing his rights and freedoms while the public seems content with the informational abuse which we daily consume from the latter.

We all agree that it's time for government to become accountable and limited. When and if that occurs, if our news media remains as it is, there's a good chance that the "man in the street" will never be informed.

Ruby Ridge Guilt

(September 28, 1997)

THE TRAGEDY AT RUBY RIDGE, culminating in the needless death of a fourteen year old boy and his mother, has recently been endorsed by our federal government in Washington and at the State level in Idaho. This recent Justice Department decision, along with the findings of a local prosecutor in Idaho, presents to the American public a frightful precedence. Rather than being a rallying cry for "right-wing extremists" or militia members, Ruby Ridge should be an alarming wakeup call to all free Americans.

The official whitewashing of the tragic and illegal actions from five years ago follows a dangerous trend that is becoming all too frequently sanctioned by Washington. Apparently, with this recent finding, it has now leapfrogged into the State of Idaho.

Recent legislation and judicial rulings from our nation's capital has reduced our Bill of Rights to that of being a prime target. Already, our First Amendment rights concerning freedom of speech have been drastically altered through this politically correct hoopla. Also, attacks continue against our right to self protection, against our freedom from illegal search and seizures and now, against the threat of double jeopardy. The original intent of other amendments remain precarious as judicial revision and/or reinterpretation rears its ugly head.

While the unconstitutionality of these initiatives remains unquestioned, the 1990s has produced law enforcement procedures which not only resemble the precision and tactics of a military operation but have resulted in scores of innocent civilian deaths. All of which our government condones! If these actions do not alert our citizenry, then what we take for granted will soon slip away.

Ruby Ridge is unique in that it presents the public with two individual and clear actions that easily point to the culpability of authority. Both incidents should come under intense scrutiny since they necessitated the violation of the most basic of law enforcement procedures. The age-old tenets of "excessive force" and the standards that permit the use of "deadly force" were inexcusably ignored and/or expanded.

The American public learned what excessive force meant when viewing the Rodney King episode. The use of deadly force is limited to the area of self-defense and for the protection of another life. This applies to both police and citizens. A thief cannot be legally shot in the back while leaving a property. However, this is exactly what happened to Randy Weaver's fourteen year old son. His wife was shot and killed while holding her newly born infant.

In the case of the boy, although members of the U.S. Marshall team attempted to say that the shooting was accidental, since he was not seen, the "accident" defense was revised so that the boy's death was the result of a shoot-out. Either position should require additional investigation since he was shot in the back.

On the following day, FBI sniper Lon Horiuchi targeted Kevin Harris as he was running towards the Weaver cabin. Incidentally, Mr. Horiuchi's career choice seems to be a case of under achievement since he is a West Point graduate. Now, citing a "split-second decision," Horiuchi missed his original running target and killed Mrs. Weaver. Curiosity should now come into play concerning his "split-second" reference. If his target was the man running, he had more than enough time to shoot. However, if his sights were focused upon Mrs. Weaver, that "split-second" reference makes more sense since, at some point, Harris could have blocked his view of Mrs. Weaver.

When facing the fact that Horiuchi intended to and did use deadly force on a target running away from his position, the results from his action cannot be dismissed. Neither the original or the mistaken target posed a threat.

At the federal trial of Kevin Harris and Randy Weaver, who were acquitted on the charges of murdering Marshal Degan, recorded testimony reveals the revision of the normal usage of deadly force. It seems that an order was issued to "shoot any armed adult."

This revisit to the forbidden landscape of illegal and amoral orders was previously trampled through with the My Lai massacre and the ensuing trial and conviction of Lt. Calley. However, this precedence had little effect upon the Justice Department's decision not to file charges against the sniper. Either from bureaucratic fumbling, an above the law mentality or just plain denial, the final decision states, "willfulness on Horiuchi's part in the killing of Mrs. Weaver could not be established beyond a reasonable doubt."

Common sense should eliminate any consideration of "willfulness" when compared to the responsibility and assumed accountability of a professional sniper. If authority deemed it necessary to use Horiuchi's talents, it must first be undeniably legal and justified. The life and death reality of a sniper's job description must be held to a higher accountability than, "Oops, I missed!"

Contrary to the gray area of trying to prove Horiuchi's "willfulness," was the local county prosecutor's findings in the death of the young boy. The report stated that the boy's death "has been determined to be a justified homicide based on self-defense." It seems that a normal usage of deadly force justified his killing since it involved a shoot-out. Still, shooting someone in the back obviously strains the legality of self-defense.

The original charge against Randy Weaver was that of selling an illegal shotgun. His failure to appear in court should not justify over four hundred heavily armed agents surrounding his home with military like precision. Normally, a second court summons would suffice or maybe the issuance of an arrest warrant.

Ruby Ridge should not only awaken America as to the innocent loss of life but also to the final conclusions which are despicable if only judged by their calloused and uncaring nature. However, equally important is the warning shot it presents as to the possibility of deadly force being abused in the future.

As a follow-up, that same county prosecutor seems to be covering all the bases. Denise Woodbury has filed not only an involuntary manslaughter charge against Horiuchi, but also a first degree murder charge against Harris in the death of Marshal Degan.

Since Harris was previously acquitted on the same charge in federal court, the fear of facing double jeopardy, being tried twice for the same offense, does not apply. It seems that the State and Federal governments are considered independent sovereigns for legal purposes.

One must wonder why our Founding Fathers forgot that "independent sovereigns" concept when they wrote the Fifth Amendment. But then, what would they think about the Ruby Ridge travesty and the need to prove "willfulness?" And to think, they got upset because the British taxed them to death!

Clinton's Reality

(August 23, 1998)

THE REFRAIN "NO OTHER PRESIDENT has had the resilience to bounce back from adversity such as Clinton," should, in itself, cause Americans to question this ability. What separates him from the former accountability and high standards expected and subsequently exhibited from this position of leadership? The answer is sadly available for all to see.

Clinton's greatest asset resides in his staunch support from the tens of millions who identify with his former days of protests against our Vietnam effort. This segment relives their rebellious past through the validation of his Presidential election. This, in defiance of the current three piece suits which adorns their middle aged bodies. While many former college protestors have since matriculated into and accepted being part of "the establishment," many have elected a president who they still connect with their younger years of idealism and carefree pursuits. They continue to condone his preoccupation with the opposite sex as both proof to his abilities and his continued adherence to their former days of unlimited freedom and irresponsibilities.

Examples for their unwavering support become indefensible against a series of questionable events from Clinton's personal and official conduct. In the face of these plausible facts, the lack of public indignation confounds.

Consider the lack of public reaction to the firing of the travel office personnel along with the ensuing false charges filed in support of such actions. Or how about the president's inability to name who hired his White House chief of security. This embarrassment was considered as an inconsequential concern. Remember when his Administration illegally obtained over nine hundred raw FBI files, which was finally explained as a "bureaucratic" mistake? This mea culpa was accepted in spite of its immeasurable political advantage and its obvious abuse of power.

Then there's always the ludicrous finding that Vince Foster committed suicide while volumes of evidence which challenge that conclusion went quietly into history. Commerce Secretary Ron Brown's untimely death in a plane crash conveniently eliminated his pending testimony at a congressional hearing concerning his Department of Commerce office.

This Clinton resilience factor extends far past political loyalties since proper public reaction or condemnation has been adversely altered.

Prior to Clinton's emergence onto the national scene, the Gary Hart episode echoed a sense of caution back in Arkansas.

As a result from an illicit weekend, which the press rightfully revealed, Hart's resignation from his Presidential aspirations may now seem a bit premature, when now gauging the public's apathetic nature concerning these Clinton indiscretions.

However, at the time of Hart's downfall, Clinton came within a whisker of entering the race. In Roger Morris's essay entitled, "Partners in Power," Morris writes, "the Hart scandal and withdrawal threw him and his campaign into a fearful paralysis. 'What happened to Gary Hart scared the hell out of him,' said one State House aide."

Why such a reaction? Through the many years as governor, Clinton had amassed a lengthy list of indiscretions, some of which even remained nameless. His bid for the White House was delayed while his staff attempted to minimize such possible sources of embarrassment. Today, as president, his apparent decision to continue with such reckless behavior reflects either an air of superiority or an inability at self control.

While Clinton's indulgences continue to make headlines, another aspect of this person makes his accountability a necessity.

As president, he tends to view America and its future on the same level that he devotes to his women. Recently, this became obvious concerning his foreign policy regarding China. Regrettably, this action is shaping into the possibility of his committing treason.

A few months ago, a CIA report surfaced indicating that China has missiles aimed at American cities. Sadly, the technology and equipment for these weapons came from America and much of it was cleared for shipment through the Clinton Administration.

On May 13th, Congressman Curt Weldon, a Republican who has not only refrained from public comment about Clinton's personal affairs but has many times supported his initiatives, gave a speech on the floor of the House concerning national security and the transfer of missile technology to China.

Rep. Weldon stated, "Mr. Speaker, this scandal involves potential treason, and, if . . . the facts are true as they have been outlined in the media reports, which we are currently trying to investigate, I think will require articles of impeachment."

The actions of the current administration have directly damaged our national security and altered the balance of power worldwide. Given this development, one must wonder why the American public still finds the need to rally support for Clinton's personal indiscretions.

It is now clear that the President of the United States has defiled his marriage vows. If proper attention was given to his Chinese policies, his oath of office would share the same lack of devotion. The seriousness of this undeniable transfer of highly sensitive technology should overshadow media reporting of his sexual infidelities.

While our news industry would claim partisanship as the motive for Rep. Weldon's lengthy congressional speech, citing such motives represents a disservice to the nation since it obscures, to the point of condoning, the more important possibility of presidential treason. All Americans must consider what events had to have occurred in order to contemplate such a critical and anti-American possibility.

Can freedom loving Americans continue with reminiscing about their youthful escapades to the point of identifying Clinton as their one link to their past? How many excuses can we offer for this "good ole boy" president?

Presidential admiration should be based upon leadership and not on our propensity to rationalize. Our original love affair in 1992 continued through our blind stubbornness in 1996. Let's not compound our misguided devotion by dangerously ignoring this questionable reality.

Seeing Beyond Media Outcry

(December 18, 1998)

A CRUCIAL ELEMENT TO THE maintenance of American freedom and individual liberty has been recently marginalized. Suffice to say that our former free and unbiased press has now taken on the appearance of an institution devoted to supporting a predetermined agenda. This unfortunate possibility is the only logical conclusion to this "knee-jerk" public reaction which was produced by another saturating campaign on the pages of our media dailies.

Such a response was created from the combined efforts of our highly esteemed syndicated columnists, nightly TV news commentaries and finished off through the additional TV product of "investigative" news specials. This almost venomous onslaught singled out the wasteful disregard for public monies with regards to the independent counsel's investigation of President Clinton.

While this "issue" continued to qualify for headline exposure, another tax expenditure, of far greater magnitude, received mere passing notice and little public response. Incredibly, the American public continued with their heated debate over Starr's $40 million expense while at the same time, Washington saw fit to vote away $18 billion to the sinkhole known as the International Monetary Fund.

Simple mathematics will show that while the press was diligently informing our citizens as to the flagrant spending of Starr, they somehow overlooked the importance of a sum which was 450 times greater and which was earmarked for the oversea bailouts of foreign economies!

Once again, our media tends to minimize the Constitutional responsibilities assigned to our elected officials. Through its agenda of misdirection and generated hoopla, the public's response begins to represent the core elements of a working democracy. It also validates our Forefather's guarded fears from such a divisive form of government. Instead, they correctly chose to implement the structural tenets of our Constitutional Republic.

Our Forefathers realized that a "democracy" is predicated upon what is often, an emotionally charged majority rule, as is exemplified by the actions from a mob. Its very nature is destructive of our individual rights. Our Republic is fortunately secured upon constitutional law and our individual rights are acknowledged to be "inalienable." In other words, the rights of all Americans were endowed from their Creator at the time of their birth. This noted Forefather stipulation places our rights "above the mischief of man," and most importantly, above the government of man.

Our Constitution is the supreme law of our land. Its rigid structure can only be approached for change through our Founding Father's amendment process. Equally defined is our impeachment format, which is in place to correct defective and/or corrupt leadership.

Since our Founding Fathers held an inherent distaste and distrust for any of the heated public sentiments holding sway over proper decision making, this recent objection against Starr's expense is irrelevant, as it should be. As this will no doubt continue from the media's instigating measures, the inference implied is that the public has developed a disliking against any thoughts towards impeachment.

The charge of perjury is an effective tool assuring court testimony adheres to the truth. Without this expectation, our judicial process takes on the appearance of a "kangaroo" setting. The enforcement of perjury is thus necessary for the integrity of the process but also, as is the case with enforcing all other crimes, for preserving our understanding that no one is above the law. That includes presidents!

If Congress opts for the easy road, refusing to impeach, they will very likely be in violation of their own sworn oath of office. If this be the case, a lowering of standards, along with public esteem will place part of our federal government under public rebuke.

When a free society places conditions upon maintaining truth as its foundation, that same foundation begins to whither from within. There can not be exceptions to the law if the law is to be respected and obeyed.

Its now evident that our President, in addition to perjuring himself, also lied to the American people twice on national TV, in a most blatant and insulting manner.

From the ashes of this latest and greatest Clinton episode, the public may well be nearing its infatuated limits. If so, can we assume that this renewed self-respect would generate heat for Congressional action?

This possibility will never be the subject for televised debate. But then again, this may conjure up reasons why it's also referred to a "the boob tube."

Unenforced Gun Laws

(July 11, 1999)

CONTRARY TO THE "SPIN" REPORTING which has become ingrained with today's journalists, the House defeated the latest gun measure for one very good reason. There are already thousands of laws restricting gun purchasing, ownership and usage.

Government seems to operate with a mindset that legislating a law solves the problem. The enforcement of said measures never quite qualifies for equal consideration.

Before echoing the outrage that has enveloped our nation's headlines, Americans must take a step back and consider this preoccupation to legislate additional gun measures without any follow-up. It's that simple. Passing another gun restrictive law might garner additional back home votes but it remains a "paper tiger" without proper enforcement. If we could duplicate out DUI effort, or maybe that is not the best comparison, this preoccupation with additional pieces of signed papers would disappear.

Rep. Gephardt termed the House vote, which defeated this latest gun measure, an "abomination." Really? Partisan politics was again cited as the root cause for such a failure. Republicans were depicted as not caring for the welfare of our children. Quite a stretch when consider that parents exist on both sides of the aisle. Gephardt seemed intent upon dismissing the need for Congressional unity as he remarked that "Republicans can't run a one car funeral."

Common sense should tell the American public that when there are already roughly 20,000 enforceable laws on the books, which deal with responsible gun ownership, Gephardt's reaction is not only immaterial and counterproductive, it represents a public display of grandstanding and over the top accusations.

In the last few decades, a most dangerous practice has evolved with regards to particular legislation. Such measures seem to be an emotional response to an event or tragedy. The most decisive period of this century, the Vietnam era, was legalized from our heated response to an incident in the Gulf of Tonkin. Today, without the blinders of emotion, there is serious evidence which questions the entire event.

Following the tragic events at a Colorado high school, emotions have again become heated through a media saturation which highlighted every inconsequential detail of the tragedy. This emotionally charged atmosphere led Congress to attempt passing another gun law, primarily for public appeasement.

Was it reported that the teenaged murderers responsible for this senseless loss of life violated at least eighteen laws that pertain to legal gun ownership? Obviously, laws are not a consideration when one intends to commit a crime.

As irresponsible as Gephardt's statements were, they became over shadowed by that rock of integrity and honesty who resides in our nation's White House. Clinton's response to his latest disappointment at trying to completely disarm the law-abiding public seemed to resemble a cheerleader's plea when he said "the American people will not stand for this."

Mr. Clinton's response, although inciting, is only wishful thinking. While his fascination with disarming the American public seems to be more lasting than most of his policy positions, he has targeted for elimination our most guarded and revered Second Amendment. America's Founding originated from our Forefather's cherished protection of their arms and ammunition stash. Our basic freedoms and individual rights are protected from tyrannical abuse because of the armed citizen.

Contrary to the theories spouted by gun control advocates, our Founding Fathers did not recognize our inalienable Second Amendment rights of self protection because they had to hunt for their dinner or defend against savages. No, their intent was to provide themselves and future generations of Americans with the right of defense against government's historical inclinations for growth, abuse and tyranny.

This eventuality, based upon the whims within human nature, lays bare the ridiculous argument that automatic weapons should be illegal. Our Forefather's believed that government had to be held in check by an armed citizenry. This fact would preclude any argument against weapon ownership, then or now.

As next year will bring to a close an American chapter in which new horizons were defiantly breached by our President, his emphasis on gun restrictions without any regard for enforcement, reminds some of his veto against the Partial Birth Abortion Ban Act in 1997. Remarkably, just two days later, Clinton designated Oct. 12th as National Children's Day. Clinton began his dedication with the words, "With the birth of every child, the world becomes new again . . ."

His talent for double speak seems applicable with his concern for the public's safety verses gun ownership. But simply defined, gun restrictions hamper personal safety by its inescapable infringement element. What's that quaint Second Amendment phrase, "shall not be infringed?" Seems that this entire gun debate may well be a case of political and illegal double speak.

Rocker And Political Correctness

(February 11, 2000)

ENTRAPMENT IS DEFINED IN GEORGE E. Rush's The Dictionary of Criminal Justice as, "inducing an individual to commit a crime he or she did not contemplate, for the sole purpose of instituting a criminal prosecution against the offender." John Rocker might well have been a victim of a similar entrapment scheme.

While in the private confines of his vehicle, Rocker was induced into revealing his most private societal observations. Realizing Rocker's rural, country-style rearing, which compared with today's strict and suffocating standards of political correctness, often represents our last vestiges of frank, open and honest discourse, the Sports Illustrated interviewer sensed the potential public reaction from Rocker's honest reflections.

Rocker's "off the cuff" remarks were obviously the product of his emotional button being set off by the normal New York city traffic and its abundance of bad and aggressive drivers. It is apparent that this interviewer played to his agitated state of mind. Since we all have our own "hot buttons," how rational would our responses be when irritated?

At fault behind this controversy is the entire anti-American premise entitled "political correctness." Its formula actually calls for a higher level of public sensitivity and somehow raises its defense and importance over our First Amendment rights of free speech. In former times of not too long ago, the average citizen's reaction would either entail ignoring or laughing at this supposed offender and his personal opinions.

During this two person question and answer drama, the most responsible participant was the one initiating the interview, not the one answering honestly.

There is little question or doubt that as the queries continued, the popularity of this piece was quickly assumed and was expected to produce higher sale numbers due to Rocker's rare insight of what "normal" is or should be.

Too often, this type of advantage taking becomes the norm of journalists conducting interviews, especially with controversial figures. The clutter brought about with the "human interest" angle offers the journalist a convenient umbrella for a questionable practice.

Political correctness stymies free speech in that it nurtures a selective area for indignations. Recently, the public was brought to a fevered pitch by the media's coverage of a military tradition of "slamming" or "punching" badges onto the individual chest of graduates. This ritual acknowledged one's qualifying acceptance into the U.S. Navy SEALS. Since the quarter inch length of the badge's pin would obviously pierce the skin, the reading public soon learned that this custom was considered "inhuman."

The uproar got to such a degree that the Secretary of Defense actually called a halt to the entire graduating procedure.

Can we objectively compare this tutored concern for members of our military verses the indifference we shower upon our own teenaged children? Consider that the industry of body piercing and tattooing is largely supported by those too young for alcoholic beverages. Also, in many cases, these services are paid for either by mom or dad. Where is the public's outrage over young teenagers wearing nose or eyebrow rings? They had to initially hurt! More importantly, what has happened to the quality of parenting and their former over used word "NO!"

This art of selective punishment is also in force within the confines of baseball and its self righteous commissioner, Bud Selig. The American public, including Selig, remained remarkably quiet while Ted Turner, the owner of the same baseball team that employs Rocker, publicly ridiculed the Pope and religion in general. This lack of response upset many since prior to Turner's gaffes, Cincinnati Reds owner, Marge Schott, received a suspension from baseball for a similar voiced offense.

With regards to our President, editors lined up across the nation to place their printed words upon adultery rather than detailing the more important evidence which may have necessitated a charge of treason. Also inherent with the media's "sleaze factor" emphasis was their subtle inference of the public's complicity when comparing our common link to adulterous behaviors. It was generally thrown about that we all are human and like Clinton, "who is without sin?"

Since we all understand that "sex sells," adultery won out verses the intricate and often boring prosecutorial details from a charge of treason. Sports Illustrated followed the same line of reasoning when deciding to publish Rocker's inconsequential opinions. The inflammatory nature of his replies equated with the probable increase in sales of that particular issue.

This episode revolves around the sanctity of our First Amendment to the Constitution. Either we respect and defend every person's right of free speech or we will lose it. In Rocker's case, his idle dribble occurred within his privately owned vehicle and with all the normal expectations for privacy. The interviewer had a professional responsibility to isolate the emotional material from his pertinent queries about the game of baseball.

Before the American public responds so quickly and judges so severely, we all should take a moment to tidy up our own messes. How many of us have been unhesitant when giving the "middle finger salute?"

Taken one step further, suppose a local news team, out searching for a "human interest" report, caught your salute and proceeded to air this emotional, embarrassing yet instinctive response on its nightly newscast? One's reputation would instantly take a hit, based upon an instantaneous and unthinking reflex.

We all have the capacity to offend and Rocker's frustrations were only answers from an exasperated human being. Since political correctness doesn't allow for such, it might make sense to scratch this off the "to do" list. We would be better served with a return to a time when we could all laugh at each other and feel better for it.

Commitment To U.N.

(April 17, 2000)

FOLLOWING WWII, AMERICANS WERE LED to believe that the United Nations offered man's best hope for peace. After well over fifty years of recorded failures, highlighted by Korea and Vietnam, the American public has paid their fair share for a dream that never materialized. Our country's continued membership in not only an inept organization, but one that has drastically altered our governmental structure, is both foolhardy and dangerous.

This perspective is supported by the August 10th 1962 observations of former President Herbert Hoover, who originally urged America's ratification of the United Nation's charter. Hoover recognized the U.N. had failed to offer a remote hope for lasting peace while "it adds to the dangers of war which now surround us." This appraisal came at a time when our Vietnam effort was still in its infancy.

The U.N.'s Secretary General, U Thant, provided what should have been an uneasy evaluation of his organization's goal of peace when in April, 1970, he remarked that the Communist dictator Lenin's ideals of peace were "in line with the aims of the U.N. Charter." Lenin defined peace as an absence of resistance to communism.

In view of these ominous warnings, what is it that compels our federal government's continued and determined association with such an inept and expensive sham? Just last year, 8.8 billion taxpayer dollars were allocated for various U.N. initiatives and peacekeeping missions.

Both in lives and dollars, Korea and Vietnam top the list of our country's U.N. affiliated actions. Equally disconcerting is the manner in which our government commenced each effort.

Truman bypassed congressional authorization as he deployed our military under the auspices of our U.N. commitment, which erroneously was believed to supercede our Constitution. Truman's secretary of state, Dean Acheson, stated on July 29th, 1950, that the purpose of the war was "to uphold the sanctity of the Charter of the United Nations."

By today's standards, Truman's constitutional disregard is commonplace, as presidents routinely commit our forces to the dictates of the U.N. This illegal authority began as a U.N. requisite, and as such questions the need of our country to remain in an organization with such an obvious contempt for our Constitutional form of government.

To study our country's history regarding our military accomplishments with our Constitutional integrity, one cannot help but notice the drop-off, which parallels our membership in the U.N.

From a U.N. perspective, wars have been eliminated. However, this only pertains to the terminology employed. Starting with Korea, America's effort was referred to as a police action or more commonly, a "conflict."

Along with the elimination of war came the natural or unnatural, depending on one's U.N. perspective, elimination of victory. Conflicts would now be resolved by peace negotiations rather than a proper American victory. As was the case with America's might in both Korea and Vietnam, victory would be removed by a series of military restrictions that in reality aided our enemy's morale and increased the loss of American life.

Pertinent to understanding this U.N. revision of warfare are the quotes from the opposing field commanders of the Korean conflict.

After Truman relieved him of his command, Gen. Douglas MacArthur reflected upon this strange and limited warfare, "I realized for the first time that I had actually been denied the use of my full military power to safeguard the lives of my soldiers and the safety of my army."

The Chinese commander, Gen. Lin Piao, later admitted, "I never would have made the attack and risked my men and my military reputation if I had not been assured that Washington would restrain Gen. MacArthur."

Both statements point to the complex and the counterproductive U.N. policies in Korea. This reliable testimony reveals that, while the American commander was restrained, the enemy's general was encouraged to engage our forces.

Vietnam followed the same undeclared route. A timely Gulf of Tonkin incident provided Washington with a justification to commit American forces on a dominant scale.

While there is a proud tradition of enthusiastically supporting all our nation's war efforts, what caused public sentiment to change so drastically? Historians now blame the anti-war mindset against the war's undeclared status. Few realized that the U.N. mandate, which supposedly eliminated America's Constitutional duty to declare war, embroiled that sentiment.

The U.N.'s authoring agent in Vietnam was the Asian military alliance known as SEATO. It was the sister organization to the North Atlantic Treaty Organization, commonly termed NATO. Instead of the legal steps required by our Constitution, namely, a congressional declaration of war, President Johnson alluded to SEATO for his justification.

In concert with the restrictive military policies, which handcuffed our huge advantage of advanced military hardware and superior fire power in the field, there was the little known fact that under the SEATO/U.N. auspices, all major military offenses required prior approval by the U.N. Security council. The obvious is clear. There was a very good chance that communist communication with various communist held UN leadership positions, warned our enemy well in advance.

Politicians repeatedly echo the refrain that the U.N. provides an opportunity for discussion rather than settling differences militarily. So far, this reasoning or advantage remains to be seen. Citing this as a great benefit for averting "conflicts" is fine but passé in this age of advanced communications.

It is time for the American taxpayer and our elected leadership in Washington to conclude that the U.N. has been a total failure. Since its first day till the present, the world has not experienced one single day of peace. On this record, we now watch as it leap-frogs into its World Health Organization and other areas of global concern. From any perspective, there is not one reason to support our continued participation in this anti-American and anti-Constitutional organization.

Public Schools vs. Home Schooling

(February 19, 2001)

BOTH THE FEDERAL BEHEMOTH KNOWN as the Department of Education and its current dysfunctional public school system are on borrowed time. Too many parents have weighed the options and decided to shoulder the responsibility and sacrifice that home schooling requires.

This growing popularity of home schooling parallels the recent educational emphasis to instruct grade school-aged children about social issues which parents continue to grapple with. This detour from basic education is nothing more than a social engineering attempt to instill a questioning anti-American bias which will hinder one's ability for mature and objective thought in later life.

Consider the social issues being presented in our public schools. Should grade school children be expected to understand or even ponder over the intricacies of "environmentalism?" Isn't it enough to wrestle with multiplication tables or develop proper penmanship? Is their time for innocence being short changed through grade school sex education lessons? Where is the need or even the appropriateness for learning about "alternate lifestyles at age ten?

The decision to discard the phonics reading method, which has been in place for thousands of years, eliminates the co-called stigma of failure. Today's progressive instructors firmly believe in and follow this "look say whole language" approach. The results have been a dramatic drop in basic reading skills.

Woven into this socially engineered form of education is the obvious assault upon the family structure, with particular emphasis against parental rights and responsibilities. This growing awareness for children's rights, defended through the façade of eliminating child abuse, introduces questions concerning not only who will teach, but who shall have authority over the child.

Imagine the mixed message to our young when the public school system champions its Drug Abuse Resistance Education program know as DARE, while at the same time, it disperses the psycho-active drug Ritalin to students with "behavioral or attention problems."

The seriousness associated with this drug is of a nature that the Army will not accept an enlistment by a high school graduate who has recently taken the drug. The Army's position is in response to data suggesting its possible mind altering influence.

A common misconception, probably intended to intimidate a parent's preference for home schooling, is the theory that only college educated parents, most notably those with degrees in education, are qualified to home school.

A recent study revealed that a parent's level of education has little effect on the home-schooled children's educational performance. Test scores remain between the eighty and ninety percentiles, whether their mothers have a college degree or did not complete high school.

Colleges and universities now recognize that home-schooled students are generally best prepared to meet the demands of higher education. Even the military and its service academies have changed its policies towards home schooled graduates.

Public school students are out performed by home schoolers by thirty to thirty-seven percentile points in all subjects. This indisputable record of achievement comes as a welcomed trade-off to the sacrifice required by parents. It also validates that money will not solve our educational dilemma since home schooling budgets operate on far less than the $260 billion spent on education during the 1993-94 school year.

American history and traditional values have undergone change through this indoctrination of "multiculturalism." George Washington is now considered to have been a racist while modern-day subversives become models for our youth. Christmas is now referred to as a "Winter Holiday" while Easter is assigned "Earth Day" status.

When this anti-American agenda is coupled with the lowered results from a public education, the option for home-schooling becomes a "no-brainer."

In 1983, the National Commission on Excellence in Education produced a report entitled A Nation at Risk. It warned that "the educational foundations of our society are being eroded by a rising tide of mediocrity that threatens our very future as a nation and a people."

Contrary to current theories, child rearing does not require a village and the education of that child should not come from an illegal federal entity. For learning, all that is required is the natural love and guidance which parents give forth.

Foreign Aid Wasted

(June 17, 2001)

SINCE OUR CURRENT PRESIDENT ACTUALLY remembers his campaign pledge to reduce taxes, this rare opportunity affords the American public with valued insight into congressional priorities. Bipartisan agreement only seems to occur when voting for foreign aid programs or for a Congressional pay raise. When the subject of a tax reduction is introduced on the floor, endless political bickering often centers upon the fearful prediction of a Social Security collapse.

Recent headlines detail "unprecedented party discipline" which brought the House into passing a tax reduction of $958 billion. The emerging political rift predicted a climate which "could poison prospects for future compromise." It has already been suggested that our "public servants" in the Senate will wait until the summer before addressing this pending rebate.

This unabashed example of Senatorial indifference stands in stark contrast to their 99-0 vote which approved the payment of well over a half a billion dollars in back dues to the United Nations. When considering the yearly expense for America's military support of the many U.N. peacekeeping missions, such a bipartisan vote is as ridiculous as it is insulting.

Senators continue to be at ease as our military was dispatched to Bosnia for a six month deployment five years ago. American taxpayers spent over $20 billion dollars for the first three years alone! When realizing the total mismanagement of our military and the huge cost for supporting U.N. policies, which are outside our military's Constitutional purpose, this unanimous vote verses their so-so attitude towards tax relief should be infuriating.

Last October, Congress passed a $14.09 billion foreign aid bill that defies logical or necessary spending. Once again, both Houses of Congress produced a bipartisan agreement.

American taxpayers are now confronted with a $963 million bill regarding child survival and disease prevention programs around the world. Also in our tax grab bag is $135 million for "emergency disaster aid" to South African nations. Americans are known for their generosity but should our humanitarian efforts come as an official expenditure within our annual budget? Once receiving the official stamp of approval, it's oh so hard to retrieve that allocation.

There is also a questionable "$127 million designated for "peacekeeping operations." Certainly, this is a miniscule amount when considering our Bosnian demands.

Elevating the ridiculous is the military expenditures to both Israel and Egypt. While $1.9 billion is earmarked for Israel, Egypt gets gypped with a paltry $1.3 billion. And it doesn't stop with the military build-up as economic aid comes in at $840 million while again, Egypt is slighted by almost $150 million.

For too long, both foreign aid and U.N. expenditures remain as expenditures without one worthwhile result. America has followed a "fool's errand" in that she has tried to buy her friendship for well over fifty years. As a country that only produced victories, until the U.N. came into existence, American taxpayers have come to believe the U.N.'s claim that it would bring peace around the world. This foolhardy management of the American tax dollar must be redirected if only for the immense drain that it produces on both our federal budget and those of the individual family.

In almost knee-jerk reaction, the single income bread winner has gone the way of the horse and buggy as dual incomes are now required to keep one's head above the financial waters. The cost to the splintering of the family structure has produced a rippling effect to societal order as parental authority is often missing.

Government, never letting an opportunity slip away, has eagerly filled this parental void as it creates service upon service to administer its caring influence. And when foreign expenditures return for congressional consideration, bipartisanship will become its fellow traveler once again.

At one point in our country's history, our public servants were considered "statesmen." Now, the highest regard rendered is "politician." The difference is as enormous as is our national debt.

Declaration Of War In Order

(October 22, 2001)

ONCE AGAIN WASHINGTON SEEM TO prefer the cart in front of the horse. What is so vile about an official declaration of war? For almost two weeks, news sources were in unison with their determined refusal to even mention this legal requirement. Likewise, politicians from both sides of the aisle remained equally rigid with their anti-declaration stance.

This stubborn anti-Constitutional position is a direct affront to their sworn oath of office. The caliber of this defiance calls into question their overall Constitutional regard. If this is their indifference, with American lives hanging in the balance, what is the Constitution's future?

Many Americans alive today were not around to experience our nation's last declaration. A day after the surprise attack on Pearl Harbor, Congress declared war against Japan. A few days later, Congress again declared war, this time against Germany and Italy. Those who became famously regarded as America's "greatest generation," fought and sacrificed while sure of being supported. This reassurance came from a Congressional declaration of war and from the fact that a totally committed nation and its citizens were in their corner as the result of that declaration. The war effort at home had a constant companion as rationing severely limited food, gas and clothing products. The sacrifice was shared.

Since that victorious effort, American GI's have fought and sacrificed without such a level of support. And, America has never achieved victory during this "declarationless" period.

During this time, Washington has mustered forces to fight communism in both Korea and Vietnam. Korea was such a pressing demand, coming on the heels of our WWII victory, that veterans from that World War were

65

once again called upon to possibly make the "ultimate sacrifice" while Congress, without precedence, refused to declare war.

Roughly a decade later, LBJ gave his solemn word to spare no effort with our defense of South Vietnam. Of course, this was from the same President who campaigned that he would not send American boys off to fight in an Asian war. However, his dedicated "effort" didn't include asking Congress to share in the war's burden by placing their name on a declaration piece of paper.

The atmosphere in our country was quite different during Vietnam than it was when the equally bloody Korean effort was being waged. Many realized the hypocrisy from being drafted while Washington refused to declare war. As was the case during Vietnam, obviously without the protest intensity or the draft, we are currently experiencing another peace movement at home during this Iraq deployment. And as was Vietnam, Iraq comes under the heading of "undeclared."

During those years of turmoil and protest, some defended their ant-war stances with the excuse, "when the Viet Cong attack America, then I'll fight." Well, guess what peace-lovers? American has been attacked! More importantly, someone should inform those patriotic members of Congress.

It's odd that these peace organizers ignore the scope of this present day threat. No longer will the struggle necessarily take place in some far off and God forsaken land. New Yorkers have long since dismissed the notion that "it can't happen here" or "it will not happen to me." At this point, the only avenue leading to peace is the inescapable sacrifice which it will cost.

These quick formations of these peace movements should reinforce the need for an official declaration of war since the present legalities permitting such disarray at home would be strictly defined and curtailed. More to the point, it would serve notice to our enemies as to our unrelenting commitment for victory.

A declaration of war sets the stage for either victory or surrender and defeat. The peace negotiations which concluded both Korea and Vietnam would never even be a possibility.

The most responsible job description of Congressional members is their awesome duty of deciding when to legalize and commit our military to war. Another generation is now charged with our nation's defense. We should not commit this "all volunteer" military as if they are members of a foreign legion. We remain directly connected to their mission and sacrifice since they are our sons and daughters.

I've seen what the American military can endure and accomplish. I've also seen the effects of not fighting for victory.

Although not all of the 9/11 victims were American, make no mistake, our country and way of life was and remains the target. For too long, the United States has been hampered by the confusion and red tape from international agreements and most definitely by our U.N. membership. The fact remains that Korea and Vietnam were authorized by U.N. authority. It didn't work then and it will not work now. What has been proven is America wins when her intent is victory. Our military deserves no less.

Kids Are Learning U.N. Principles

(January 6, 2002)

IF A CERTAIN PUBLIC EDUCATION program is allowed to continue here in the Sunshine State, American pride and patriotism will be on borrowed time. In all likelihood, this indoctrination of the young is taking place in many school districts throughout the United States. Safeguarding the impressionable minds of our nation's youth must be addressed and maintained.

Back on October 15th, it was announced in the local paper servicing Daytona Beach that a United Way event would feature an official representing the U.N. Association at a luncheon to discuss "the U.N.'s involvement in the war on terrorism." Apparently, there exists a local county chapter of this international organization that meets monthly. Obviously, this should have little to do with public education. Not so! The conclusion to this article showcased the reach of influence that this misguided association has produced or at least expects.

To briefly quote, "In addition, the high school Model United Nations, where students engage in discussions about world peace, environmental global issues and terrorism, plans future mock Model U.N. conferences at the following locations." An associated listing of five dates, at five different area high schools, followed in this local paper.

At what point does America's foolish involvement with this inept U.N. organization warrant high school attention to world problems that continue to stymie world leaders? I fully realize the value that Hitler placed with his programs to channeled "education" for the next generation. This modern day curriculum, while conspicuously lacking the proper studies of American history and civics, apparently does not deviate from that dogma.

As expected, the October 27th newspaper issue ran an article detailing the luncheon discussions. A Mr. Jeffrey Laurenti, who heads the Policy Studies of the U.N. Association, cited the difficulty in defining the difference between "freedom fighters" and "terrorists." The inability to separate these two distinct functions may well define the U.N.'s inability to accomplish any worthwhile goal.

Our Forefathers remain as the world's most successful examples of "freedom fighters." They fought to gain their native country's independence from a foreign oppressor. Terrorism operates for the purpose and goal of creating public hysteria and fear through mass destruction and needless loss of life. Quite a difference and easily explained.

Throughout its half century of existence, this U.N. consortium has failed miserably at being "man's last best hope for world peace."

Essentially, our school-aged children are being taught U.N. principles, rather than gaining the necessary understanding and pride which a detailed American history course would provide. Ours is a glorious and colorful heritage and is jammed packed with heroic leaders throughout every chapter of our country's development. With this global instruction in place, is there any wonder at to why home-schooling has become so popular and productive?

Time has come to restructure school lesson plans to an American format, that is not only instructively useful and nationally productive but one that ignores such distant and irrelevant dribble.

It's also time for our country to disengage from an organization which has continuously promoted leadership loyal to the socialist/communist venue since its creation. The U.N. has seen its day. School districts across the nation should see the same reality and agree.

The future of our nation lies with those who are in today's classrooms. We as loving parents and patriotic Americans are not being faithful to our national sacrifice if we continue to turn a deaf ear to this global propaganda which masquerades today as public education. If we love our children and our country, our course is clear.

Smoking Issue

(June 6, 2002)

WHAT TO DO WHEN A reduction in State revenue increases the expected $677 million shortfall to $1.1 billion? Politicians being what they are, the remedy will always center upon the portion of voters with the least political clout. In this case, it's the helpless smoker.

The ease to which government can target responsibility toward a certain minority is supported by the overwhelming majority's applause when a "free ride" appears on the horizon. This is the perfect example of how a democracy works. It also provides clear reasons why our Founding Fathers opted for a Constitutional Republic.

In a democracy, those singled out are without individual rights. This is exactly the plight of Americans who decide to smoke. Few recognize the threat from a government which endorses a policy based upon pitting one American against another.

Consider this anti-smoking craze. It began with the sectioning within commercial jet aircrafts. Just like the introductory amounts of income tax, look what it festered into. Lost in this shuffle is the clairvoyance of common sense. The concerns surrounding secondary smoke, which has been determined to be just a bunch of smoke, has never-the-less become a vehicle for oppressive legislation which the career politician endorses just because of the numbers represented.

Gov. Schweiker's hot air would have us believe he is more concerned about the ability to stop teenagers from buying cigarettes than finding an ample source for State revenue. Maybe, but such compassion is a rarity in the political arena whereas revenue greases the gears.

Please do not insult the smoker with such heartwarming intentions. The intelligence and sense of fair play has marginalized the anti-smoking crowd through greedy expectations and the euphoria which comes from imposing one's will upon another.

If we listen to those who represent the "smoke-free Pennsylvanians," one hears that smoking endangers the lives of the innocent. This is pure nonsense! Their main objection to secondary smoke is their valid perception, based upon their personal dislikes, that the aroma is not only unpleasant but it also is a nuisance.

Desirous of living in a pleasant and near as possible perfect world by only respecting their own individual "pursuit of happiness," these Americans have banded together in a coordinated and well financed voting block to coerce the average vote hungry politician into trampling upon the rights of the law-abiding smoker.

I might add that not all non-smokers agree or support this doctrine of "might is right." Some non-smokers make up the age old "exception to the rule" adage as they remain quite comfortable in their favorite smoke filled taverns and inns. In fact some voice embarrassment concerning the radical non-smoking fringe as their insistence to force their will upon others is unrelenting.

It is this radical element of any social cause that continues our social divisions, suspicions and unrest. It may well be that an absence of protest could very well crumble their identity and/or sense of self worth.

I would like to applaud a Mr. Bill Godshell, who represents the group, "smoke-free Pennsylvania." One will never hear a politician voice the honest reasoning behind this latest cigarette tax increase. Godshell remarked, "You need to get revenue, and they are going to go to the least opposed revenue source."

One question begs for an answer. If, in fact, the revenue "shortfall" is fueling this limited tax oppression, why is it that politicians from both sides of the aisle are already suggesting that the spending from this additional revenue be earmarked for the State's prescription-drug program or to "increase health coverage for the uninsured?" Sounds more like a budget surplus than the advertised "shortfall."

While my observations may tend to offend the majority, my intention is to present a rare yet needful consideration within a free society. Since I bring to the table experience from both sides of this issue, being a fifty year smoker who quit, I recognize and concur on points from both positions; especially those individuals with breathing difficulties. Again, my main concern is with the ever opportunistic politician who spends revenue like "crap through a goose."

At this point, the question of a budget "shortfall" or "surplus" becomes secondary to the unity of our nation. When legislation centers upon making each smoker's puff more and more exorbitant, the nuisance is not solely relegated to the aroma issue. There is another stink present!

Make Politicians Accountable

(October 3, 2002)

FORGIVE MY SKEPTICISM BUT I have heard the war rhetoric before. I even believed it. That is, until I witnessed the results from American sacrifice.

In my day, it was a leader named LBJ. His war became so difficult that he couldn't even muster a run for re-election. War is hell!

Today, our "leader" is a man named "George W." For a year, America has conducted a ghost-like war against terrorism. Today, without any concrete evidence as to the fate of Osama Bin Laden, we are beginning to ratchet up America's fear against Saddam Hussein's possible use of "weapons of mass destruction." Who would argue against preventing such a devastating possibility?

Let's assume that such weapons are available to Hussein. We can also assume that his "madman" tendencies heightens the threat. Why then is it so important to seek United Nation approval for action which directly defends and protects our country.

For too long, Americans have taken for granted that those we elect to the presidency have somehow developed the rare blessing given to the few who can handle such weight. For over fifty years, our presidential "leaders" look first to gain United Nations approval prior to any foreign military commitment. This is not the act of a leader. Nor is it the act of an independent sovereign nation. Leaders do not ask! They decide!

War may impart somewhat of a cavalier notion since our recent military efforts have resulted in comparatively low casualty rates from our high-tech weaponry capabilities. Is America prepared or able to return to a ground effort, which is more costly in terms of lives?

In the aftermath of Vietnam, wars are waged by venues, which offer the least amount of casualties. The political fallout resulting from Vietnam-like casualties have shifted our dedication and military efforts.

This was the case with our reluctance to rid the world of Hussein over ten years ago. Today, we seem eager to reverse our course and finish the job. The question remains: Is the American public ready for such loss of life, but more importantly, are politicians ready to wholeheartedly support our military with a congressional declaration of war?

If anything was learned by our Vietnam sacrifice, it should be the need to first legalize our effort through congressional support. However, this logical first step is being avoided "like the plague" since those in Congress have little desire to uphold the responsibilities of their office.

Vietnam proved the fallacy of war without an official declaration. The reason that this Constitutional requirement continues to be ignored is simply because our government has transferred its authority and solemn responsibility to the foreign entity known as the United Nations. It is that organization which will condone military operations and decide when it is fitting to stop the exercise.

Most importantly, the possible "war" with Iraq will not end in victory but with the United Nation's mode of a "peace settlement." In short, America may commit its forces yet not have total command or authority. Just as was the case in Korea and Vietnam, this will be a U.N. "conflict."

These words of concern will contradict most of the U.N. propaganda that has become so prevalent within our global society. It may be upsetting or even unbelievable, since we've become a nation of listeners instead of questioners. However, it's the truth!

In my day, a President said, "ask not what your country can do for you, ask what you can do for your country." We did! Our country asked and those of us who were called, answered. We responded to a war which military leaders confirmed could be and should be won within approximately three months. That is, if America fought the war to win. This estimate was based upon the sole use of conventional weaponry. With the U.N. involvement and control, it took ten years to lose!

If war with Iraq is a must, let it be decided in Washington and officially approved with a declaration of war. Make our politicians as accountable as those who are charged with the war's costly reality.

One constant with American "leadership" links the Vietnam era with today. Corporate boardroom bigwigs ascend into responsible positions, who in times of "conflict" voice the most hawkish of views. My generation was guided by a Robert McNamara. Today, Dick Cheney is once again fluttering those hawkish wings. It's amazing that McNamara and Cheney have achieved military clairvoyance without ever experiencing any of the wartime uncertainties of a buck private.

No, the rhetoric of war has not changed and neither will our sacrifice gain victory until Congress finds its Constitutional backbone.

Trent Lott's Miscues

(December 27, 2002)

I DON'T LIKE TRENT LOTT! In fact, I don't like many of our elected "leaders." However, what I really don't like is this selective and self-righteous indignation based upon irrelevant babbling.

Comments made at a birthday celebration should be left at the birthday party. Just as the off-the-record conversational comments from John Rocker lack relevance to a sports oriented interview. In both cases, our media seized the politically correct dagger of personal destruction. All with the public's supportive appetite.

This public reflex to the media's targeting of individuals is as dangerous as it is un-American. We used to be a thick-skinned society. Contrary to the politically correct crowd, many Americans harbor assorted prejudices. After all, what is a prejudice other than a personal preference? Our opinions, right or wrong, form our likes and dislikes. In order to act with a politically correct manner, are we willing to be mentally neutered?

Returning to the Trent Lott scenario, he is hard to defend since his calling in life is automatically suspicious. The success of a politician depends upon his ability to "go along to get along." Often, personal ethics and principles take a back seat to headlines and political party agendas. The identity of "statesman" has largely disappeared from the Washington stage.

Having stated all this anti-Lott jargon, let me make clear that this current racial sensitivity is very selective and closed minded. While we all should be well aware of Sen. Bryd's equally insensitive remarks of a year ago, we somehow dismiss his past indiscretion as irrelevant history. The integrity of racial harmony becomes suspect as we continue to gloss over

Sen. Bryd's former Ku Klux Klansman involvement. The same reaction holds true for Rev. Jesse Jackson.

In 1994, Rev. Jesse Jackson preferred the term "hymies" when referencing the Jewish population of New York City. He also took the liberty to rename the city "Hymietown." Although this direct insult was covered by the media, it obviously lacked this current intensity.

My point, where is the consistency? Where is the 'fair and balanced" portion of the news? This one sided emphasis lacks any resemblance to a "free press," let alone a "fair and balanced" one. If our dander is up by Trent Lott's stupid utterance, where was that dander in 1994 or last year? Certainly a former Ku Kluxer's use of the "n" word should be worthy of such infuriated coverage.

As I said, I do not particularly care for Sen. Lott nor do I respect his senatorial performance when I review his sworn oath of office to "preserve, protect and defend the Constitution of the United States." And sad to say, he is no better than the vast majority of those we elect.

Presidents, members in both Houses of Congress and those un-elected power and policy brokers at the cabinet level positions generally treat our law of the land as an "outdated" hindrance. To those such as Lott and Bryd, not only has your mouth proven your lack of integrity and dignity, your open disdain for the limitations placed upon our government attests to your priorities and self-importance.

Without realizing, the popularity of our "on again off again" fairness and balanced criticism includes the tarnishing of societal integrity and decency. We become puppets of media stimulus. We properly react when singing the media's pre-orchestrated chorus. Our thought process is now based upon emotionalism rather than common sense and logic.

Through this media dissertation of Lott's foolish remarks, a political motive begins to evolve. If Lott can be insulted and humiliated enough, there is a chance that he will not only be replaced as the senate Majority Leader, he just might feel the need to leave the public limelight since it will continue to follow him as a senator. The governor from his State happens to be a democrat. If Lott takes the easy way out and resigns, the realignment of Senate control would be assured. Who can't say that this possibility keeps the media heat at its current high level?

To paraphrase a recent and gifted politician's defense of his own immoral actions, "who is without sin?" Or how about, "no attack ever fed a hungry child."

While unfortunate, Lott's remarks come from the same trough that others sample. Until every remark can receive equal media coverage or more importantly, until Americans can once again find the ability to laugh at themselves, then common preference will always be viewed as a politically correct prejudice.

U.N. Claim Bunk

(March 30, 2003)

INITIALLY, PUBLIC FEAR AND INSECURITY were the main ingredients causing our acceptance for joining the United Nations. Promoted as the world's "last, best hope for peace," our usage of atomic weapons during the closing stages of WWII shocked many into believing that only a world organization could prevent the future of wars using atomic weaponry.

This current U.N. stalemate of the Iraq issue clearly demonstrates that the U.N.'s ability for maintaining accord with all nations through its offering of an "international forum" is simply global hogwash! After fifty-plus years in existence, the U.N.'s record has consistently produced petty bickering among its member nations, secret alliances which often endorse an anti-American socialist position, but more importantly, a reversal from it originally stated purpose of maintaining world peace.

By an ironic reversal, the U.N. now represents a world level of authority for commencing war. Without public notice, this about face has been in play almost from its beginning.

It may seem unthinkable but this organization, designated for ensuring world peace, began flexing its military might with the authorization of America's defense of South Korea in 1950. Both Korea and Vietnam were U.N. authorized "police actions" or if you like, "conflicts." They were never "wars" since the U.N doesn't recognize such and American leadership has since chosen to ignore its Constitutional responsibilities. Instead of producing victories, these exercises were constrained and ineffective as when one washes his feet while still wearing his socks.

Since this entity is without allegiance to America, or even to any particular nation, the age old goal of military victory is counterproductive as it tends to inspire national pride and patriotism throughout the victorious country. Therefore, to begin with a tie, was preferable in Korea and a loss was even better in Vietnam. That is, from a U.N. perspective. This Vietnam loss deflated American pride and patriotism and at the same time, adversely effected America's reknown institution of unity.

It is now insultingly clear that the U.N.'s purpose for achieving and maintaining world peace is nothing but a sham. Since its creation, the world has not enjoyed one day of peace. Still, this organization somehow receives the attention and respect as if it were incredibly successful.

Our nation's half century of associated U.N. misdirection and false expectations may best be summed up with this hard hitting headline, "U.S. finds support scarce at U.N." This news item reported that "urgent diplomacy" failed to gain the nine required votes on the Security Council, which would endorse an American initiative with regards to an Iraqi deadline.

This intrigue at the Security Council gets better as two "crucial swing votes" for giving America permission to proceed are none other than the world dominating countries of Chile and Guinea! Now if this does not infuriate and reduce the importance of the U.N. to its incompetent and counter-productive setting, what will?

Also to consider is that the U.N.'s head spokesman, Kofi Annan, warned the United States "it would be in violation of the United Nation's charter if it attacked Iraq without Security Council approval."

Since when does the U.N. charter supersede our United States Constitution? The United States would never and could never create an organization with superior authority over its own law of the land.

Given our experience during Vietnam, the fundamental step of proclaiming a declaration of war should now be verified as a legal and necessary step for maintaining domestic unity through obedience to our Constitution. Also, it's an essential recognition of honor and support for the unavoidable military sacrifice which our Country will endure.

As freedom loving Americans, now is the time to question our continued dalliance with such an unattainable world concept. In addition, its threat to our constitution is a menace well worth addressing. Our military has undergone a disservice of which parallels the U.N.'s existence.

Many Americans have served and sacrificed without any realistic hope for achieving victory. This is an immoral and disgraceful result from our irresponsible creation. And to think that American Presidents have been swayed by its global allure almost from its first day.

Our Forefathers believe that man was meant to live in freedom. Our continued apathy, with regards to this growing U.N. shadow, questions their basic premise. Now is the time and place to answer the age old query of, "is man's true destiny one of freedom or enslavement?" Let's hope we prove it to be the former choice rather than the latter.

Oblivious Congress

(June 10, 2003)

THE DWINDLING AMOUNT OF AMERICAN corporations which have remained in this country have been busy "cleaning house" for the last twenty years under the guise of cutting the corporate fat. Recent actions in the House of Representatives should call for a political version of this corporate trimming.

On May first, this august body representing the American taxpayer, approved a measure, by a 375-41 vote, which allocated $15 BILLION to combat AIDS in Africa. The downsizing of Congress, as tempting as it may seem remains legally impossible. However, our recourse from this betrayal of public confidence and faith will be best served in the voting booths of 375 Congressional districts.

For too long, the game of politics has shielded selective indignations and hypocritical grandstanding by political hacks. Any accommodation for common decency or public respect, when spending the taxpayer's hard earned money, has been lacking since our Nation last enjoyed a balanced budget. This was verified within an accompanying article detailing this illegal expenditure, reported by the Washington Post.

The Associated Press, reporting on the proposed elimination of taxing corporate dividends, quoted the concerns of Rep. Charles Rangel. He actually had the audacity to state, no doubt fueled by his political agenda, that, "People are hurting. They are afraid of losing their jobs, losing their health care, having to take their kids out of daycare." Of course, this tirade was meant to portray such a plan as just another White House scheme designed to benefit "wealthy investors."

Rep. Rangel's outrage came on the same day as the House voted on the African AIDS legislation. Somehow, this representative is upset about

82

reducing or eliminating taxes on invested money yet is comfortable with legislating 15 billion dollars to a foreign country. This is just the latest example to the sad quality of representation which hard working Americans have been duped into electing and re-electing.

If, as Rep. Rangel mentions, the American "people are hurting," how can 375 representatives of "hurting" Americans be so cavalier with such a large portion of their taxes? It's ironic, if not incriminating, that those same representatives previously allocated roughly the same amount, $14.9 billion to this year's foreign aid give away.

Such behemoth financial expenditures seem to reduce the significance to the parade of lesser outlays which often remain unreported. However, these seemingly trivial amounts form a pattern validating a sad human tendency which could be defined simply as "who cares?" Consider the following Congressionally approved budgetary items.

Federal tax dollars were spent for a $2.8 million fish farm in Stuttgart, Arkansas, $1.3 million to repair a privately own dam in South Carolina, $49 million for a rock and roll museum, $7 million to study air pollution in Mexico City and $375,000 thousand to upgrade the House of Representative's beauty parlor. And sadly, this is but a very abbreviated list of our Federal Government's irresponsible use of our hard earned tax dollars. This is the nature of the 'good ole boy's" corral of back home "perks" and "pork barrel spending". Obviously, these amounts are only "lesser" with those who spend other people's money. To the average tax payer, the sums are very real and substantial!

When considering that our National budget is approximately six trillion in the red, these unlawful yet "lesser" expenditures become part of the problem when totaled.

The argument that America must be sensitive to the needs of countries around the world may be a valid consideration if our economy was healthy and jobs were plentiful. "Globalization" has cost millions of American jobs as our industrial base has been decimated.

This trend has now infiltrated among those who have obtained college degrees in the computer science field. Third World computer technicians are being imported through a corporate process known as "outsourcing." Of course, this popularity for foreign workers is incentivized through a 20 to 50 percent reduction in wages.

It seems that in today's world, all fields of American endeavor are subjected to the economic belt-tightening from corporations. All except for the insulated field of politics. It is absurd that career politicians have an open checkbook which the American tax payer continually strives to balance.

By their own example, changes in House personnel are needed to fairly represent the American public. To further underline this growing need, check the political harmony when the next Congressional pay raise surfaces for a vote. If this does not insult the public into action, then our "hurting" is only another political ploy by self feeding politicians.

Ten Commandments Defense

(August 24, 2003)

I JUST DON'T GET IT! Why all this controversy over a 5280 pound Ten Commandments monument in front of the State Judicial Building of Alabama? Alabama Chief Justice Roy Moore is correct by refusing the removal of that monument.

Let us remember our founding Declaration of Independence against Britain's increasing oppression. Our Forefather's wrote, "we hold these truths to be self-evident, that all men are created equal, that they are endowed by their Creator with certain unalienable rights."

Each of us begins life with our rights bestowed, not through our federal government, but from our Creator. America's basis for freedom is found in her recognition of these blessings from a higher authority. Therefore, religion is embedded within America's social fabric and political framework.

That declaration's closing sentence acknowledges once again what current standards are trying to erase. It states: "And for the support of this Declaration, with a firm reliance on the protection of Divine Providence."

Of course, current standards may cause some to find the end to that sentence equally uncomfortable.

Consider our Forefathers' degree of commitment with the words: "We mutually pledge to each other our lives, our fortunes, and our sacred honor." Their belief in their cause was no less than their subsequent written intentions.

In the Bill of Rights, the First Amendment opens with these words: "Congress shall make no law respecting an establishment of religion, or prohibiting the free exercise thereof." That signified the importance of religious freedom to our Forefathers. Somehow, we have mutated this right to the point that prayer and the mention of the "G" word are no longer permissible in public.

It is interesting to note that there is more pertinent information and knowledge in what is not mentioned or studied than with what is. Aside from Thomas Jefferson, George Washington and James Madison, how many other Founding Fathers do we recognize? Benjamin Franklin and Alexander Hamilton are faces on our currency. Some may have heard of Gouverneur Morris but what of James Wilson? How about Fisher Ames of Massachusetts? Morris was the most vocal member at the Constitutional Convention and Wilson was his close second.

As I said, what is not mentioned or written can often be more educational than the spin of misdirection and the fluff characterizing our current editions of America's "free press." Let's consider the contributions and quoted beliefs of those unfamiliar Founding Fathers.

Governor Morris was in charge of the committee responsible for the Constitution's final wording. Intensely familiar with the Constitution's intent, a "separation of church and state" is never mentioned. In fact, Morris is quoted as saying, "education should teach the precepts of religion and the duties of man towards God." No wonder that this particular Forefather remains ignored, especially in the realm of Supreme Court rulings.

Then there is James Wilson, of Pennsylvania, one of the original Supreme Court justices who was appointed by President Washington. In his writings he states, "far from being rivals or enemies, religion and law are twin sisters, friends and mutual assistants." His relevance is further strengthened by his authorship of America's first legal text on the Constitution. Interestingly, the phrase "separation of church and state" is not mentioned. Again, is there any wonder as to why modern Supreme Court rulings ignore Justice Wilson?

Finally, there is Fisher Ames, who may be considered our First Amendment's author as he provided its final wording. This should qualify Mr. Ames as an authority on that Amendment's intent. As such, he also fails to cite a "separation of church and state." In fact, he believed that the Bible should remain as the most important textbook in the classrooms of our young nation.

Throughout the years, the original intent of our Founding Fathers has been denigrated by unconstitutional legislation and questionable judicial rulings. This systematic revision to our Constitutional pillars has been greatly aided through the misdirected curriculums so common within current public educational formats.

Consider that most patriotic citizens believe that America's form of government is a democracy, when in reality, it is a Constitutional Republic. The word "democracy" is not mentioned in our Constitution or Bill of Rights. This is an outright falsehood which practically every modern day politician repeats and repeats! Why?

The tendency of the media is to portray Judge Moore as slightly overzealous and leaning to the right. Whatever slant he may possess is not of the right or left persuasion. It is towards our Constitution and in the defense of individual state sovereignty. Instead of questioning his hidden motives, we should all be thankful for his proper stand and Constitutional allegiance.

Now consider the liberal leaning Supreme Court Justice William O. Douglas' words in a 1961 ruling. "The institutions of our society are founded on the belief that there is an authority higher than the authority of the State; that there is moral law which the State is powerless to alter; that the individual possesses rights, conferred by the Creator, which government must respect."

There is unfortunately a reason why many of our Founding Fathers continue to be ignored. Justice Douglas's 1961 words will never be a legal cornerstone for present or future Supreme Court rulings. However, it could provide the pivotal point for all free Americans to say "enough is enough!"

Lack Of National Resolve

(December 10, 2003)

IT'S ONE THING TO FACE the possibility of death when serving one's country. It's quite another to train for a one time mission which requires one's death. Americans considers this to be fanaticism. Reality suggests that it is the last resort brought about by the overall economic and military disadvantage of those who choose to do battle with America.

This last resort type of thinking was evident with the Japanese kamikaze pilots during the closing months of WW II. Like it or not, that ultimate example of one's loyalty had to evoke a sort of amazed respect by those who watched their dying efforts. This level of sacrifice was also a tactic employed by the Viet Cong, as sappers would blow themselves up in order to breach an American perimeter.

Today, we may consider such actions to be a radical alternative, often induced through drugs or false promises of martyrdom. Whatever the reasons or causes, America is left to combat an enemy who is at peace with his coming sacrifice. At such a level of commitment, we are obviously at a disadvantage since our forces can only react after the fact.

This is not meant to criticize those in uniform or belittle their sacrifice. Never! Those from my generation, myself included, who wore our Nation's uniform during time of war, shared the same dedication, honor, sacrifice and respect with those currently serving and sacrificing. Their loyalty and will to win is not in question. What is being scrutinized and condemned is the degree of dedication from our elected public servants and those unelectable policymakers who remain shielded from any physical danger or personal sacrifice.

As was the scenario in Vietnam, our military might is being marginalized by guerrilla type tactics which operate and depend upon initiating the action. To offset the demoralizing effect which comes from the enemy's ability to pick and choose the place, manner and time of action, our forces must be supported to the max. Our refusal to declare war sends an unmistakable signal to our enemy.

In addition to this "iffy" war effort, which those terrorists living in caves and tunnels fully appreciate, America's weakest link is her public's intolerance for sacrifice. This was the lesson our enemies learned from our "peace with honor" in Vietnam.

This comparison of wills, those of our enemies verses ours, must also take into account the disparity between the military options by the "bad guys" verses our controlled and limited military strategies. This is mainly due to our heightened concern for those innocent civilians who may be caught in the crossfire. Obviously, the "bad guys" have a huge advantage, since their military edge is to initiate battle without any thought for civilian losses.

Without realizing, even acknowledging the term "terrorism" or "terrorist" strengthens the terrorist agenda since its usage implies that a degree of concern, or at least an awareness, exists within the American public. That is a major goal of a guerrilla fighter. Terrorize the countryside, or in this case, far away America.

Not meaning to belabor a point but I believe our military record during the last fifty some years proves the need to address what Washington refuses to consider. Committing our Nation's military to war must begin on a solid and unified footing. Such decisions must be in accordance with what our Country's law requires. That is, a Congressional declaration of war. Not only does this step legalized our actions and officially honor our inevitable military sacrifice, it sends notice to our enemies that trying to amass public opinion against our efforts will not be tolerated. This is crucial when considering war as a last alternative. To ignore such a legal step automatically implies that our intentions will be halfhearted at best.

Our current conflict is not isolated to a third world country half way around the world. Without a firm dedication to victory, from both our elected leadership and our general populace, our efforts will ultimately be in vain. Consider our Nation's insufferable arrogance when attempting to rid the world of terrorism yet refusing to secure our national borders.

The need for our Country to officially declare war should be obvious. America wins when war is declared. America loses when it goes to "war" without a declaration. It's that simple. And it's that sad, since those in uniform still willingly sacrifice their youth and noble beliefs.

Globalization Threatens America

(April 18, 2004)

BEHIND THE MASK OF "GLOBALIZATION," is an American enemy solely intent upon transforming our nation into a state of dependency and economic despair. The sad, yet necessary participants in this strategy are the greed-driven American corporations which seem blessed with endorsements from our federal government.

This harsh and even frightful assessment will most likely be difficult to consider, much less believe, since it very well could encompass that which we have been taught to mock, the ridiculous "conspiracy theory." As we watch America's downward slide, can we afford to cavalierly dismiss such a premise?

We're not just losing jobs. We are deporting America's ability to maintain and provide her essential needs for tools, machinery and military parts and even to maintain her technological capabilities and leadership. This future of dependency will include the sacrificing of our freedoms, our individual rights, and of course, all of our opportunities. Our individual options will be nil.

If this sounds far-fetched, consider what we have already accepted in the agricultural field. For years, we have imported food while our country remains the world's most plentiful and agriculturally rich country in the world. Why? Importing produce from Latin American countries, grown in conditions other than with our high American standards and requirements, is ludicrous since our government continues to subsidize American farmers not to grow. This we have come to accept, while at the same time, feeling justified with our "conspiracy" ridicule. Who would have envisioned this insane scenario fifty years ago?

Also ponder at the ease at which Americans have come to believe that the world in general, and America in particular, is in the midst of adjusting to the changing world of technological advances. We are being lectured about the next century's focus on the information and service industries. Can we say "hogwash?" Where is the job security if the skills required are that of making a bed, waiting on tables or taking reservations.

How does the most powerful country in the world, the country which represents the most freedom and individual opportunity, maintain her status as a world leader and protector if our booming industries are service and information? Interesting to take stock in what other countries are experiencing this economic downturn? The answer is, America leads!

So, our economic survival is now on the bargaining table. Next year, another bit of the puzzle appears as our national sovereignty comes into question.

Few of us are familiar with the letters, FTAA, translated it stands for, Free Trade Area of the Americas. Our president wants this "free-trade" treaty in place next year. The greatest chance to defend America is to pressure Congress into voting against such anti-American legislation. This is just an enlargement to the North American Free Trade Agreement, NAFTA.

After ten years, the promises from NAFTA have resulted directly in the loss of approximately 900,000 American jobs. Instead of the prediction that it would strengthen our borders, the reverse has taken place, as our border integrity has disappeared.

If this FTAA legislation passes next year, it will enlarge NAFTA's three countries—United States, Mexico and Canada—to the grand total of thirty four and, thereby, increase the trade pact's power and control. Our United Sates will become a "member state" in "the Americas," in the same manner that European countries are earmarked for the same nation-losing status.

Since America is still the land of opportunity, why is it that our government sees fit to allow and even encourage this outsourcing? We need to see the total picture of what is taking place.

Instead of judicial endeavors against Martha Stewart's stocks-related crime, our courts should be jammed with both ranking governmental officials and CEOs facing the charge of economic treason!

Women In Combat

(April 23, 2004)

OUR FRONT PAGE NEWS IS now informing Americans about the death of a female soldier, one of three soldier-sisters stationed in Iraq. Enough is enough! The only other military force which routinely used women in combat was the Viet Cong. Is this to be the criterion of our Country's military?

Very serious questions must be addressed. I don't care what the equal rights agenda says! It is not necessary for American women to die while serving in our military.

Can anyone say the word "infidel?" In the Arab world, this is our identity. Right or wrong, their treatment towards women is often described as inhuman yet it excludes any military tour of duty. By our standards, they are repressive, insulting and abusive. If we are to gain their support and trust, is America putting her best foot forward by fielding a female inclusive military force?

Another consideration centers upon the public's change of attitude from the threat of a draft verses the indifference of a volunteer force. This point is pertinent since there is current talk of resuming some sort of draft. The overseas commitments, along with the changing demands placed upon the Reserve and National Guard units have caused this talk of restarting the draft. If such a possibility becomes reality, support for our war against terrorism will definitely undergo a radical redress.

If the draft is initiated, shall women be eligible? There is a world of difference between a committed women's decision to volunteer and quite another to have one's daughter receive her "greetings" from Uncle Sam. The nature of this equality is unnecessary, insulting and will be socially damaging.

One does not have to be a male chauvinist to agree that since the beginning of time, men have protected women. Like it or not, it's the natural order. Men's abilities offset women's shortcomings and women's abilities offset men's shortcomings. Hence, marriage works if and when each respects and relies upon their mate's special abilities. One could make the point that our military experimentations into sexual equality reflect or may affect our growing divorce rates.

The other side of the equation of male protection is women's nurturing abilities. Providing the patience, understanding, comforting and the tenderness that men often seek or may require are special God given gifts. So often, a woman's love and understanding can ease a man back from war's shocking experiences. Now this ageless formula will change as women experience unnecessary exposure to combat.

Can we picture the husband or boyfriend at the airport waiting for his combat hardened wife or sweetheart to return home? Can we envision his unnatural role to comfort or to understand his wife's experience and sacrifice? What is wrong with this picture? And please do not try to say that this is exaggerated or ridiculous. We as a Country have yet to experience the social repercussions caused by women returning from combat.

Is it possible that military training can erase the natural instinct to protect a woman, even one in uniform? And what of the physical attractions and the physical capabilities verses the physical demands of combat? This experimentation into sexual equality has increased the associated dangers with soldiering.

The media attention given to Sp. Michelle Witmer's death defines the continuation of the different coverage when an American female soldier is captured or killed. This special attention inadvertently points to the unnaturalness of placing female soldiers in combat positions.

This particular tragedy has especially touched me since both Sp. Witmer and I were MP's. I am very familiar with the uncertainty and vulnerability from "pulling convoy duty." Vietnam is history and especially so since our Country has failed to learn from its mistakes. Yet, I can remember the vigors of being an MP both in Vietnam and stateside at Fort Benning, Georgia.

I also had the experience of meeting a neighbor's daughter who was called to active duty. Ironically, she was an MP and stationed at Fort Benning. This mother of three was in obviously good shape, "cute as a button" yet weighed maybe 110 pounds. It is difficult to understand how a 110 pound MP could "hold her own" with the duties that I experienced.

In conclusion, I would like to extend my sincere sympathy to the Witmer family and pray for those who wear our Nation's uniform. I have grave fear for our military, our Nation and our society since a nation which sends its women into battle is not worthy of the contest, much less the victory.

Justice System Askew

(August 8, 2004)

THREE UNRELATED NATIONALLY RELEASED NEWS items all too accurately reflect a growing trend to interpret law as a "living" standard for enforcement. Fading into the sunset are the previous expectations to fair and equal treatment from our system of justice.

In its July 19th issue, USA Today headlines reported the Martha Stewart sentences to be of such minimal punishment that the "light term raises the stakes for an appeal." In other words, the degree of punishment is so minimal that any thought to filing an appeal would be ludicrous.

A sentence which severely challenges the advantages from an appeal is inherently inconsistent with the law's sworn duty to administer firm and reasonable punishment. This "high profile" case underlines a growing diversity within the application of justice between what is generally depicted as "the haves" and "the have-nots."

The second example, reported locally in The Daytona Beach News-Journal of July 20th is another "high profile" case as the accused is a well known professional athlete. Kobe Bryant's trial is already too high a price.

The state Supreme Court of Colorado "ruled Monday the news media have no right to publish mistakenly released details from a closed-door hearing in the Kobe Bryant sexual assault case . . ." This unconstitutional decision was defended by further unconstitutional reasoning. To quote, "In a 4-3 ruling, the high court acknowledged the order amounts to a prior restraint of a free press, which is barred by the Constitution." In what is a variation to a familiar excuse, it was theorized, "The court, however, said such a step was permissible given the context of the Bryant case."

What case "context," which remains unknown to the American public, justifies this blatant Constitutional violation? This premise is akin to the decades old state Supreme Court ruling which erroneously supported the DUI roadblock stops without probable cause. It was theorized that the added safety achieved by those measures overrode any Constitutional concerns! Now, "context of the Bryant case" supposedly justifies further disregard?

Finally, the News-Journal readership was treated to a little scandal nostalgia with its front page headline, "Ex-Clinton advisor took 9/11 documents." To that, many readers could say, "What's new?"

Again, it seems to be another rendition of "the haves" verses "the have-nots." Since Sandy Berger was formerly a Presidential national security advisor, . . . "no decision has been made on whether Berger should face criminal charges." Really?

Let me understand this. Berger "knowingly removed handwritten notes he had made while reading classified anti-terror documents . . ." Also, "He also inadvertently took copies of actual classified documents . . ." Sounds like if one is "inadvertent," one may be exonerated from criminal intent. I wonder if a bank robber could claim that he inadvertently demanded money from the teller?

Similar to his bosses defense based upon the definition of the word "is," Berger stated, "When I was informed by the Archives that there were documents missing, I immediately returned everything I had except for a few documents that I apparently had accidentally discarded."

Oddly enough, those documents "accidentally discarded" were "highly classified, and included critical assessments about the Clinton administration's handling of the millennium terror threats . . ."

Care to guess what will happen to the absent minded Sandy Berger? Forget that he was seen placing "documents in his clothing" or that he stated "I inadvertently took some documents from the Archives," some of which were "accidentally discarded."

We can complain all we want about the lack of accountable government, an illegal war or a cowboy for President. A new face in the White House will mean little if our system for justice remains askew.

Martha Stewart has been inconvenienced. Bryant will continue to draw headlines, no matter the outcome. Berger's future may entail an inadvertent probation, if charges are even made. Meanwhile, I hear that some could face years in jail for possessing small amounts of marijuana.

Even if the "weed" was inadvertently possessed!

Deterrence Factor Absent
In NFL Punishment

(January 29, 2005)

NFL DISCIPLINE GUIDELINES CALL FOR action due to "obscene gestures or other actions construed as being in poor taste." The public insults committed after Moss's second touchdown against Green Bay exhibited both "poor taste" and "obscene gestures." However, the anticipated fine is not sufficient punishment when considering that ten thousand dollars is levied against a multi-millionaire. At Moss's income level, this paltry sum is nothing more than "tip money!" The deterrence factor which is punishment's muscle is obviously absent.

For too long, football fans both in the stadiums and at home have endured watching as these celebratory gyrations grow in both frequency and time of duration. Apparently, today's professional football player considers doing his job as a boastful event. Consider what a defensive end is paid to do? Sacking a quarterback or tackling a running back behind the line of scrimmage justifies his huge salary. A wide receiver's first down catch is his job expectancy; not some miraculous achievement. Imitating the referee's first down motion is third rate and professionally embarrassing.

All this individual gloating or taunting is nothing more than manipulating national TV exposure for self promotion. As such, this should qualify under the NFL's "poor taste" criteria since it erases football's team effort concept. This self glorification has been allowed for too long. It not only detracts from the sportsmanship of football, it now sets the stage to outdo other performances. Once the curtain of vulgarity has been raised, the need to outdo or to gain notoriety will enlarge the repertoire to this obscene genre.

Equaling the crude and classless actions of Moss are our media apologists. First, to ensure that all who missed the game itself experienced the insult, morning papers across the country carried a photo of a bent over Moss displaying his mooning exhibition. Later in the day, the arch conservative Rush Limbaugh acknowledged his inability to understand the public uproar when comparisons are made to other social indignities. He apparently believes that once the bar has been raised, actions which would formally be considered insulting should be quietly accepted.

The Philadelphia Inquirer and Daily News web site asked the question, "Were you offended?" Amazing! Not only were the fans in attendance and the home viewing audience insulted, asking the question is insulting! And maybe that is the problem.

Has our society reached the extremes of permissiveness? Are insults or vulgar actions acceptable if gradually introduced? What will offend? What constitutes "enough already!"

Some apologists have condoned Moss's insults by comparing "the more insulting" escapade of Janet Jackson's wardrobe during the last Super Bowl. Also, Monday Night Football's inappropriate lead-in with Terrell Owens and Nicollette Sheridan was mentioned as objectionable.

Finally, journalistic appeasers submit that since Green Bay's infamous after game parking lot celebrations include the actual mooning of the departing visiting team's bus, Moss's clothed imitation seemed to be understandable.

How far down the scale of decency will our excuses finally rest? Are we to condone inexcusable public displays based upon the rowdy and most likely alcohol inspired actions of football fans at a frigid Green Bay parking lot? Actions which were off camera and therefore previously unknown?

It is often said that the quality of government mirrors the morality and integrity of the society it governs. Well, the same can be said for the integrity of not only professional football but all of professional sports! Need one point to the recent NBA brawl in Detroit or to the obvious greed which erased the NHL season? What about the skyrocketing home run figures which blew by previous standards which were seemingly unreachable!

I think that the point of "enough already" has long ago been surpassed. The integrity of all sports must once again showcase sportsmanship; humility in victory and graciousness in defeat. The current self promoting, taunting and now vulgar displays, which have characterized the last decade in the NFL, must be eliminated

The NFL's rule book detailing game penalties should include another penalty. Fining a millionaire a few thousand dollars is not an effective deterrence. In addition, a team being penalized fifteen yards will produce an immediate impact. Now, if we only care enough about the game to honor it with a practical and enforceable deterrent.

Secure National Borders

(May 15, 2005)

AMERICA IS RIPE FOR THE picking! Our citizens lack both understanding and respect for their inheritance of freedom and individual rights. While we amuse and identify ourselves through our enclaves of special interests and pet peeves, our government seizes every opportunity as it exhibits a lawless indifference to its limited Constitutional authority. In short, we have become our worst enemy!

From the ashes of the twin towers, a field in Pennsylvania and the Pentagon, the American landscape has been revolutionized and transformed to extremes which were previously illegal. Today, our Country is being ruled by a government which either contradicts itself when the need arises or, as previously stated, flat out operates outside the legal parameters of our Constitution. Examples are endless.

Consider that Americans who are dependent on air travel or even just choose it for their vacation mode of travel, are now being treated as possible terrorists without exception. Even little children and older ladies with walkers are considered as possible or even dangerous threats. This we permit as assurances of increased safety sooth our possible objections.

Our military now enforces the un-American policy of "pre-emption;" which is nothing more than a politically correct version of the uglier word, "invasion."

After gaining the victory over Hussein's forces, an "exit strategy" still awaits implementation. Instead, President Bush has greatly expanded our mission stating, "It is the policy of the United States to seek and support the growth of democratic movements and institutions in every nation and culture, with the ultimate goal of ending tyranny in our world."

In my day, our foreign policy was questioned since it appeared that our military adopted the role of the "world's policeman;" a reference to our anti-communist efforts in Korea and Vietnam. After the infamous failure of our Vietnam crusade, we are now somehow charged with the task of taking on terrorism on a global scale and promoting democracy wherever.

In our Country, which was born out of protest, when do we object to such nonsense? Has the disappearance of the military draft quenched our conscience or our ability to recognize that even the United States has limits with it military? Since when is democracy such a great goal? Especially when we all begin to realize that America's not even a democracy!

Of course, it wouldn't sound so inspiring to send our forces around the world to spread a Constitutional Republic. Our concept of a "democracy," which is inherently against individual rights, sadly reveals our lack of Constitutional understanding.

So while our forces are struggling to bring peace to the Middle East and Iraq in particular, Washington diligently introduces additional measures designed to avert another terrorist attack. Quite a task since we seem incapable of stemming the flow of illegals invading our Southwestern States.

President Bush is quickly transforming the American Presidency into a hemispherical President of "the Americas." He pampers the anti-American whims of Mexican President Fox rather than maintaining a secure border or even remaining faithful to his oath of office. On the one hand, law abiding citizens are "bending over backwards," foregoing individual rights, in order to comply with our government's increased safety charades at airports, yet the flow of illegal aliens continues to be ignored, condoned and even encouraged!

This unconstitutional authority is thriving within all three branches of government. Legal minds term what our Supreme Court has recently ruled as "activism," which is just another quaint term for unconstitutional action.

However, this ruling, which finds that capitol punishment for those under eighteen to be a violation of the 14th Amendment's "cruel and unusual punishment," contradicts its own 1989 STANFORD v KENTUCKY decision. That 1989 Supreme Court ruling explicitly stated that executing 16 or 17 year olds does not constitute "cruel and unusual punishment."

What caused this judicial reversal? It seems that in this global lunacy which we think of as "free trade," there also has arisen a need to infuse legal findings or standards from foreign authorities. Never mind that some wearing black robes today were the same justices from that 1989 STANFORD vs. KENTUCKY decision. This contradiction also places in jeopardy their individual oath of office to "protect and defend" our Constitution.

Enter our Congressional defenders who also have sworn to defend the Constitution. It is not just their authority but their responsibility to guard against improper conduct by members of the Supreme Court through the impeachment procedures found detailed within our Constitution.

Invalidating American law by citing foreign standards such as Article 37 of the United Nations Convention on the Rights of the Child, epitomizes the impeachable standard of "improper behavior." In fact, it's downright illegal and we are still waiting for Congress to exercise their Constitutional responsibility.

At some point, we must recognize and even fear what is taking place under the guise of legal authority. We must move past the political agitators who would continue this democrat verses republican banter. We must demand common sense government from both political entities.

Such a common sense approach may well call for redirecting all of the billions we spend in foreign aid so that our Country's sovereignty may be secured once again by a strong national border. National security begins at and is defined by our borders, not by harassing children and senior citizens at our airports!

Protecting Economy Is Foreign To U.S.

(July 23, 2005)

HAVING ACHIEVED ALL THAT HE could for India's job market and economy, New York Times columnist Thomas L. Friedman now sets his sights upon improving the minuscule economies of six Central American countries. Once again, at America's expense!

Mr. Friedman's recent editorial entitled, "Mon Dieu: Are we all Frenchmen now?" negatively compares any possibility from an anti-CAFTA vote in Congress to the rejection of the EU's constitution by the citizens of France. When will our nation's journalists feel the sting from the dwindling job market, of which they so cavalierly ignore?

One premise of Friedman's latest anti-American crusade is aimed at those American "protectionist" and their "fear of competition." Friedman applauds as "the global playing field is being flattened, bringing in more competitors from Poland, China and of course, India." At the same time, Friedman ignores the dollar amounts of foreign aid which America gives to her new "competitors." This omission obviously serves to protect the concept of "free" trade.

Mr. Friedman's entire concern seems to center around distain for the "protectionist" concept and our Central American commitment to "consolidate these fragile democracies." Hell, with an eight trillion dollar bill hanging over our economy, America should also be termed "fragile!" Still, every year, we manage to give away over $15 billion foreign aid dollars!

To address Mr. Friedman's first priority which aims at America's so-called "protectionist" policy, Thomas Jefferson stated in 1799, "Commerce with all nations, alliance with none, should be our motto." America's only experience with a "protectionist policy" was George

Washington's statement that "Tis our true policy to steer clear of permanent alliances, with any portion of the foreign world . . ." Of course, this policy opens up a bag of worms, given our 20th century history. It also questions the motives and economic feasibility for enlarging the original NAFTA agreement, which after 10 years must be considered a one way trade failure. Why support enlarging what has obviously been an expensive foreign aid package?

How can Mr. Friedman remain impervious while America's work force deals with lay-offs, and employer outsourcing to cheaper labor markets. Now add the ever increasing tide of illegal immigrants willing to work for "slave wages." From a practical viewpoint, "free" trade is nothing more than a systematic and greedy betrayal bordering upon economic treason and ultimate destruction.

CAFTA expands the economic disaster known as NAFTA with the inclusions of Guatemala, El Salvador, Nicaragua Costa Rica, Honduras and the Dominican Republic. More than fifty percent of the 46 million citizens of these six countries live in poverty. Once again, these numbers underline more of our one way trading policies, given the lack of economic strength which an importing nation requires. And the sad part is that neither Mr. Friedman nor our elected officials will reveal this as an intermediary step leading to the 34 nation Free Trade Area of the Americas, or simply, the FTAA.

Each step is presented as if it is the ultimate for increased trade when it is a quicker method for reducing America's high wages and standards of living. As with NAFTA, these agreements have little to do with free trade and all to do with foreign aid investment with our tax dollars.

This CAFTA urgency is just another chapter to our government's concern for our southern neighbors. Washington continues to act as if America is a rich and influential nation, when we are hugely in debt. Somehow, we focus upon the future of Social Security when our real priority should be our Country's overall financial stability.

Blessed with a stubborn memory, I recall Gov. Bush, the candidate, pledging "I will not nation build" when elected President. What changed? Why is it now important to help those "fragile democracies" when our Founders detested such a reckless form of government?

It doesn't require a PHD to understand the economic unbalance associated when a country's average hourly pay roughly equals a poorer country's weekly wage. Only one direction is possible and we have been witnessing it for at least the last ten years!

I suspect Mr. Friedman's view will not change until the NY Times sees fit to trim expenses by importing a New Dehli journalist. His farewell article may finally be one worth reading.

NFL 'Me Teams'

(December 18, 2005)

I'VE SEEN ENOUGH! FIRST, IT was the Monday Night debacle in Atlanta, followed by the seemingly impossible drubbing by the Dallas Cowboys. Later game losses at Denver and especially at Washington provided the inescapable reality that Philadelphia's continued dominance over the Eastern Division was in jeopardy. The Eagle's latest loss to Dallas, in Philadelphia, nailed the last nail into our football coffin.

Philadelphia is obviously in football trouble. However, from years of silent witnessing, I believe that the entire NFL is now suffering from the identical sickness which ushered our team's slide from respect. This malady, which is sadly condoned by the NFL and promoted by the various TV sport newscasters and pre-game analysts, has replaced the "team concept" with an intensified coverage upon the individual.

As the NFL has grown in popularity and TV viewing throughout my lifetime, which from a football standpoint, began at Franklin Field and was highlighted by Philadelphia's 1960 championship, big money now dictates the scheduling based upon optimum viewing time. The show business leading up to Monday Night Football is its most obvious example.

Who can remember when football was strictly an outdoor and daytime sport? For that matter, championship games were played in all kinds of weather and with capacity filled stadiums. The NFL has changed and it is not necessarily for the better!

Along with this increase of revenue, the NFL's "show business" identity first appeared with the end zone antics of Billy "White Shoes" Johnson. His novel expressions highlighting his individual abilities are now common game occurrences. Almost every play now ends with some sort of bullish, mocking or even insulting display promoting individual prowess. Today,

106

these actions may tend to increase the average player's bulging bank account as these promotional gimmicks attract advertising agents.

This aspect, along with its downside to team unity, cannot continue. The Philadelphia Eagles epitomize the inevitable results from this "me-me" mentality.

The Eagles' Nov. 14th Dallas loss on Monday night illustrates just how inappropriate are the immediate displays of self gratification. After running in for a game leading touchdown, McNabb performed a personalized version of a celebratory dance. Again, such displays have become routine for only accomplishing what a player is actually paid to do. In retrospect, McNabb's premature elation seems a bit asinine when considering that it occurred before half the game was over. Following that stunning Dallas come-from-behind victory, celebrating such an early game touchdown clearly takes on the appearance of a Philadelphia Eagle embarrassment!

Today's average NFL game is promoted and dissected by the hordes of highly paid former players and coaches. Their detail analysis of featured games may include the color of socks worn or the latest musical rendition sung by a combination of past and current NFL players. No wonder that this competitive game is now referred to as a form of "show business."

Pre-game shows also highlight and rate replays from the previous week's individual celebrations. Given this degree of attention, these acts of egotistical self promotion begin on the opening kickoff. Offensive and defensive players immediately prance around as professional wrestlers in the ring after every catch or tackle. These individual acts must be seen as immature, embarrassing and inherently premature since half of those displays will come from the losing team!

McNabb continues to break Philly hearts with ill-timed interceptions, often to a wide open defensive player! "Misreads" continue to plague this five time All-Pro. Obviously, something is amiss with our QB, but more importantly, with the overall NFL product. Maybe the NFL, with its "show business" approach, should re-evaluate football's former standards for being humble in victory and gracious in defeat.

As for the Eagles, McNabb believes that "life is a learning process." Dance steps will not produce football victories, unless it's the "dancing" that Fran Tarkington or "Roger the Dodger" performed! But then, that was before the "we-teams" turned into the money driven "me-teams!"

Immigration: An American Issue

(April 19, 2006)

CONTINUING THE ILLEGAL FLOW OF cheap labor into the United States seems more important than our obvious need to increase border security during a time of "war." This conclusion is particularly disturbing, if not outright dangerous and irresponsible, given that the very definition of terrorism is to infiltrate and then detonate.

Even without the current "war" against terrorism, unrestricted immigration presents a flurry of problems which our former immigration policy prevented. Individual communities will experience tax increases, heightened criminal activity and overcrowding of both public and social services.

Acting as if these unavoidable consequences are immaterial, the Senate's current immigration "debate" is nothing more than a crowd pleasing show prior to a close pro-amnesty vote. Wars have never, and now National security will never interrupt business or alter the "art of deal making"

Most would agree that America's twentieth century growth was mainly due to the past toils and tribulations of immigrants forging a new life as proud American citizens. However, few "open border" supporters acknowledge the fact that those new arrivals not only entered our Country legally but also met a very stringent criteria leading to citizenship.

President Bush's immigration stance has changed the old saying, "if it ain't broke, don't fix it" to, "if it ain't broke, break it!" Our President routinely cites the economic advantage and national need provided from this foreign and illegal work force. Bush is all too willing to ignore or revise our Country's immigration standards in order to "match willing foreign workers with willing American employers." Supposedly, this only applies "when no Americans can be found to fill the jobs."

What has caused this labor vacuum? All of a sudden, high school graduates are not joining the workforce. Could it be that pay rates for those entry level jobs have been lowered and thus have become unattractive to Americans?

This economic reality has effected the American job market to the point that high school graduates now join the military rather than seek safer at home employment. No wonder that a possible resumption of the draft fails as an attention getter. The illegal presence of cheap labor has devalued the work force to the degree which makes a military career financially attractive.

Washington's refusal to address causes leading to a lower working wage, which eventual will produce lower living standards, reflects upon that long ago global promotion known as a "level playing field."

Supporters of such romanticism chose to believe that its attainment would automatically raise the standards of third world countries. It was theorized that an increase in both employment and international trade within the global community would universalize economic prosperity. Few considered the other option.

Nations which were highly developed or considered as economic pacesetters, such as the United States, were targeted for a reduced global role as lower wage scales, outsourcing and the importation of cheap labor became effective leveling agents. Today, jobs which could not join the many millions exported overseas are now being offered at foreign wage levels. American's reduction of economic strength has lessened societal standards and dampened the individual's expectations for attaining success!

This issue begs for one correction. Too many "authorities" in both the fields of government and the media continue to refer to this National insult as an "immigration issue." The word "immigration" carries with it an insinuation of an orderly or legal process for the relocation of families or individuals. What is happening to America could never be described as "orderly" or "legal!" This is nothing more than foreign economic invasion, which to date, has failed to ignite a pro-American response from our leaders.

In closing, this is not a republican or democrat issue; it's an American issue! The word "illegal" must have meaning since it is the backbone to our judicial system. When illegals can blatantly conduct a rally or protest without any thought to arrest or deportation, then our Country has lost more than it's immigration quotas and standards. It has lost its governmental authority to enforce its laws and ultimately, to maintain a peaceful and productive society!

Government's POW/MIA Policies Remain Insensitive

(August 14, 2006)

ON JULY 4TH, THE FRONT page of the Daytona Beach News Journal featured an article entitled, A Soldier NEVER FORGOTTEN. What ensued were, once again, details unveiling our government's consistently insensitive and counter productive POW/MIA policies. Policies which are devoid of common sense and logic, if its quest is still the discovery of truth!

This story detailed the loss of three Green Berets while planting wiretaps along the Ho Chi Minh Trail in March 1968. In January, 2000, a Department of Defense POW/MIA discovery/recovery team excavating the area where the three soldiers were last seen discovered a single tooth which eventually was identified as the official remains of Master Sgt George Ronald Brown. It was ascertained that the tooth "compares to a radiograph of his—that is a dental X-ray."

News of Sgt Brown's tooth identification was forwarded to his daughter, Ronda Brown-Pitts of Dayton, Texas. Ms. Brown-Pitts became curious with her father's official identification when she compared his dental records with the tooth in question. It seems that the recovered tooth is without the filling which was noted in her father's dental records.

Her next step, prior to the government's intention to quickly inter the "remains" of Sgt Brown in a full sized casket at Arlington National Cemetery, was to ask for a DNA test. This was refused since it would "desecrate the body."

It seems that our military follows a convenient policy of "not doing destructive testing on the remains if that would destroy all the remains."

I use the word "convenient" since in many cases, "remains" are often that confining and miniscule in size and therefore "conveniently" off limits to such undeniable identification methods.

Supporting Ms. Brown-Pitts skepticism were the opinions from retired 1ˢᵗ Sgt Curtis Marcum, a special operations veteran who personally served with Sgt Brown. Sgt Marcum believes that if his comrades indeed died at the location of the recovered tooth, there would certainly be more evidence available. Sgt. Marcum then mentions what many Vietnam veterans believe to be the central and consistent theme to the entire POW/MIA issue. Sgt. Marcum states, "The feeling of most of us is that they are using this tooth to clear the books."

Sgt. Marcum's view is difficult to discount. Consider the record, the consistency of dismissing, debunking or discrediting the information, whether it be more than the 1400 refugee reports of "first hand live sightings," testimony from highly respected and decorated military officers which include a former Chairman of the Joint Chiefs of Staff, or an actual live walking and talking Marine POW who engineered his own escape from captivity!

Upon Marine PFC Robert Garwood's return, the government elected to discredit his person and taint any possible POW/MIA information through court martial proceedings.

Even the statements from a former President of the Soviet Union, or the pictures which identify a Special Forces Captain by the most minute facial comparisons and finally to the October, 1990 minority staff of the Senate Foreign Relations report which caused the headline, "Study: U.S. Turned Back on POWs in Asia."

Can there be any defense or explanation to that Senate report's conclusions that, "In fact, classified, declassified and unclassified information all confirm one startling fact: That Department of Defense in April 1974, concluded beyond a doubt that several hundred living American POWs remained in captivity in Southeast Asia."

Also the report stated, "This was a full year after DOD spokesmen were saying publicly that no prisoners remained alive." And this is the policy which still remains in place.

There is one verbal exchange which was made public print during the 1992 Senate Select Committee on POW/MIA Affairs, chaired by Sen. John Kerry. Quoting briefly from a June 26ᵗʰ, 1992 Daytona News Journal article on Page 3A, Sen. Kerry questions former Pentagon official, Roger Shields, who was in charge of accounting for the missing from the Vietnam War, concerning a conversation he had with former Deputy Defense Secretary William Clements.

Kerry asks Shields, "You recall going to see . . . Clements in his office, in early April, a week before your April (news) conference. And you heard him tell you, quote, 'All the American POWs are dead.' And you said to him, 'You can't say that.'" Shields replied, "That's correct."

"And he repeated to you, 'You didn't hear me. They're all dead.'"

Not to belittle or degrade such a serious matter but this exchange is reminiscent from a scene in the Harrison Ford movie, "A Clear and Present Danger."

To "clear the books," as Sgt Marcum puts it? It's been a forgotten issue ever since the last US helicopter took off from that Saigon rooftop. At this point, after well over thirty years on the books, Washington fully expects that this POW/MIA disgrace will fad away along with the numbers of those Vietnam Veterans who quietly and honorably believed in and served their Country.

THIS
ROAR
of OURS

JIM BOWMAN

There is an obvious movement taking place in America today. Its roar is unmistakable. This work is a humble attempt to identify and discuss some of the particulars influencing our Country today. Although some concerns travel back over fifteen years, they still remain pertinent and effecting.

My approach to our Nation's ailments may seem out of sync or infuriating at first, yet, isn't this reaction indicative of just how far we've strayed from our experiment of freedom and individual liberty? My point is that much of what currently ails America can be simply cured through both ample doses of individual responsibility and Constitutional allegiance. Hopefully, you will agree.

ISBN13 Hardcover: 978-1-4653-4316-1
ISBN13 Softcover: 978-1-4653-4317-8
ISBN13 eBook: 978-1-4653-4315-4

Published by Xlibris
Order Today!
Order from your local bookstore,
call 888-795-4274 ext. 7879, or order online at
www.xlibris.com, www.barnesandnoble.com,
or www.amazon.com

Xlibris
WRITE YOUR OWN SUCCESS

Level Playing Field

(November 12, 2006)

SOMEWHAT "LONG AGO," YET NOT so "far away," the concept or supposed need to establish a "level playing field" was introduced to the American public. Approximately twenty-five years have passed since that unifying goal was first introduced. Today, that "playing field" has mutated into a "global community," and/or "global workplace." Do we dare consider how or by what method that imaginary "playing field" is undergoing such "leveling?"

From a most rudimentary approach, if any economic "leveling" takes place, which first must be recognized as socialistic since it's reminiscent of Marx' redistribution of wealth belief, only one of two methods can be used. Either the living standards and economic prosperity of "rich countries," namely, the United States, must be lowered or the poorer countries will undergo an enriching metamorphose. Ever consider why that introductory term "level playing field" has disappeared from public view? Today, it is increasingly clear as to which option was utilized.

I doubt anyone thirty years of age or younger can remember the corporate need to "downsize," which also has long since faded from current jargon. It was theorized that major companies needed to "cut the corporate fat." What took place was generally a reduction in the actual workforce which was hardly a hiding place for "corporate fat!"

The next step leading America into this global community was the economical treason of "outsourcing." Billed as a way of bringing economic prosperity to poorer countries while offering cheaper priced merchandise to the American consumer, the end result is another story. Child labor, often in sweat shop environments, has grown while the American consumer is still waiting for an appreciable price reduction of foreign made goods. All the while, corporations overseas grow fatter.

Now obviously, there are some areas of employment which just are impossible to ship overseas. The solution is the current cheap labor invasion, mainly from Mexico. Not only does Washington refuse any legitimate effort to eliminate this illegal immigration problem, it actually seems to endorse its continuation! And, that is the telltale sign to this ongoing attempt at lowering America's industrial and economic power.

Proof to this seemingly wild yet sadly accurate portrayal continues throughout today's society. The aftermath of the 2004 hurricanes introduced homeowners to a massive number of foreign workers within the roofing industry. Oddly enough, roofing prices remained the same!

I recently remarked to a friend as to the benefit from the war in Vietnam being similar to Germany and Japan following World War II. My attention was drawn to the manufacturing label on expensive items of golf attire found at a local pro shop. You guess it; "made in Vietnam!"

Are we crazy? Just what does America produce anymore? We are now witnessing the slow demise of our auto industry as illustrated by Ford's huge reduction in employment. Even our navy yards have been closed in favor of foreign repair facilities. Reason? America saves fuel by not sailing all the way back to American shipyards!

How is it that America now finds the need to import meat and produce while Washington pays farmers not to farm? Do foreign producers obey the same stringent crop regulations? What happened to American lamb chops? All that has been available for quite a while comes from "down under."

Are we crazy or just lazy! Once out of high school, current graduates either enter college or one of the two "service" industries. The most financially rewarding just happens to be the military. Is it any wonder that trade apprenticeships have followed the fate of the stagecoach!

I just recently returned from a vacation to the historical bastions of Philadelphia and Boston. What a magnificent sacrifice our Forefathers endured to grant this Country its freedoms and its people their inalienable rights. Those men were aided not just by deep thought and vision, but from their mutual respect and their courageous belief for individual dignity.

As we continue to leap into this global craze, let us not forget our Forefather's main concern when creating our Constitution and Bill of Rights. It was all about curbing the basic human frailties of greed and power. And, those frailties remain the same whether one is on horseback or driving a BMW.

Constitutional Ignorance

(February 21, 2007)

WILL THE RESPONSIBILITIES OF FREEDOM ever be accepted? We have taken on the appearance of those inheriting wealth from the labor of others. We lack even an ordinary appreciation or respect for the liberties which our Forefathers sacrificed to bequeath. Thomas Jefferson warned, "Ignorant and free will never be." Few words but once again, visionary as were typically our Forefathers!

There are always those who will yell, "Not so!" Who will attack the messenger with ridicule and laughter. There will always be the few who avoid action, even as the danger beats down their door. Until recently, this "head in the sand" approach was uncharacteristic to anything American!

So, let Americans return to their former selves by shedding the chains of correctness and sensitivity. Let us take stock in the gradual degradation which has crept over our once vibrant economy and work force. Let us now and forever chant, "enough is enough!"

And for those "doubting Thomas's," who love to doubt, consider our folly without excuse making.

Throughout America's history, our foreign wars have been declared legal by first attaining a Congressional declaration of war. That is until President Truman initially by-passed this awesome and obvious Constitutional demand. The question remains, "what caused such a silence in Congress when this first was attempted" and even more curious is "what induced Truman into thinking he could by-pass our Constitution without the hundreds of Congressional members objecting?"

This indefensible violation, a violation from a Presidential abuse of power and permitted by a mummified Congress, sadly continues to the present. Remarkably, since the lack of any Congressional declaration, the

115

most powerful army in the world cannot gain victory over limited forces from second and third world countries! This defies logic!

Now consider today's generational lack of Constitutional understanding along with the disappearance of any worthwhile citizenship teachings. The same can be said about the inability of today's students to even read time from the face of a clock. Penmanship and basic cursive writing skills are also disappearing as computers engulf our daily lives.

However, America's army of social engineers will justify these adaptations as a progression, a natural order of things evolving from the rudimentary stages of our development to America's current modernization. In short, these progressives lack practical relevance!

The prevailing school of thought today is that while our Forefathers sacrificed to achieve our freedoms, the original intent to their writings is not appropriate to the problems of modern society. This revisionist viewpoint conveniently ignores the main concern and effort to our Forefather's writings. They recognized freedom and liberty's chief enemy to be the frailties and short comings of human nature. This, along with the instinct for governmental growth and eventual corruption occupied their cautious creation.

Today, signs of their long ago fears are everywhere. That fear from governmental growth has manifested itself to the point that if our current bureaucracy was reduced to its legal Constitutional size, the average amount of Federal income tax would be reduced by more than half! So, reasons to write off our Founding Father's warnings and beliefs become necessary.

The degree to which the average citizen, along with the average public servant, has drifted from such worthwhile understanding of our Constitutional freedoms, liberties and governing laws can be sadly gauged by our belief that America is a democracy when in fact it is a republic! So, why is it that our foreign policy is so adamant upon "introducing democracy to Iraq" when in fact America is a Constitutional Republic?

The repetition of a lie eventually evolves into being a truth! This is classic to the public's belief that America is a democracy. In almost campaign like fashion, the hordes of elected officials voicing this lie begins at the Oval Office, drifts through the halls of Congress and filters down into the countrysides of our local governments. And, there's little hope on the horizon.

Currently, I am reading Sen. Obama's best seller, The Audacity of Hope. This charismatic and freshly arrived Senator, one who supposedly taught

Constitutional law at the University of Chicago for ten years, somehow continues to connect or identify America as a democracy twenty-nine times within his first five chapters of his popular book.

Not only does Constitutional ignorance abound in Washington, common sense seems to have fallen from grace also. How important is it to fight terrorism abroad when our National borders are wide open to illegal entry? How many terrorists are among us?

As our government continues down this anticipated path for growth, the reasons for ignoring our Forefather's messages become very clear. Just as today's version of our "commander in chief" lacks the battle tested experience of a George Washington, Americans lack the individual initiative and love for freedom that began the American experiment with liberty.

Again, consider George Washington's pertinent description to what they initially feared as he warned, "Government is not reason, it is not eloquence. It is force. Like fire, it is a dangerous servant and a fearful master"

Yes, Mister Doubting Thomas, it has been well over two hundred years but those visionary Forefathers correctly anticipated our current dilemma, and it had little to do with modernization. It's still all about human nature!

Why Imus Paid for All Our Sins

(April 30, 2007)

DO WE NEED ANY MORE proof as to why our Forefathers feared and detested a government based upon democracy? The recent firing of "shock jock" Don Imus was a perfectly detailed example of democracy in action! Thankfully, America remains as a Constitutional Republic.

To understand the workings of a democracy, first realize that actions leading to a desired outcome or goal often become motivated through emotions. This so-called "heat of the moment" leaves little room or time for clear and/or logical deliberation. This emotional surge speeds along through the assurances from "good intentions."

At its most effective level, a democracy is nothing more than the majority rule from a lynch mob or the more respectable and legal sounding term, posse. How many old western movies have we watched where the rustler was caught and hung by good intentions? Remember the rope burns on the innocent neck of Clint Eastwood?

Just as the old west posse was formed to only arrest and not hang the bad guys, the media saturation of the now infamous Imus statement over stepped a proper public condemnation. And it was once again swept along with the emotional wave which characterizes a democracy.

From a personal perspective, I found the televised form of the Imus in the Morning show to be a laughable bore. Soon after retiring, I happened across this windblown egotist by the accident of channel surfing. I found him and his show to be a perfect example of how opportunity can still be had in America. Here, from my point of view, was an incessant talker who really loved to hear his own voice. What impressed me the most was his own infatuation and obvious regard for his considered brilliant ramblings.

And, not only had he achieved monetary success for such nothingness, his popularity survived decades!

It is no secret that in the course of a normal morning show, Imus tested the limits of free speech. Everyone was fair game. That in itself became a debilitating habit which is fed only by his continued testing of those limits. Through the years, I believe that Imus eventually considered himself to be untouchable. Especially insulated when compared to the performances of another much fouler mouthed "shock jock" who recently signed an unheard of mega deal contract.

Comparing the two, Howard Stern verses Don Imus, the latter conducts a more tame and acceptable format. It is inconceivable that Mr. Stern's vulgarities continue to find acceptance. But, there again, the emotional response targeted one goal, much in the same manner as that western posse's bad guy objective.

Yes, Imus offended, insulted and unfairly depicted a college basketball team of young female athletes. In today's super sensitive society, I fail to understand both his humor or his reasoning. However, I am embarrassed by his knee jerk firing. In no way do I condone or support what was said on his morning show. He deserved condemnation and punishment. He received the proper condemnation and in retrospect, improper punishment. Should firing be part of his sentence while other formats go unchecked? I think that our own miniature cleansing was in part paid for by Imus. Now I think it's time for us to return our heads into the sand and hope everyone forgets our uncontrollable rage.

The word rage might be offensive but consider the similarities to those cowboys on horse back. At one point, when advertisers ran away, when front page headlines and endless talk/news shows replaced Iraq with an easier victory, there was a sense that "the blood was in the water." At that point, the rage of correctness carried to the final outcome.

If indeed "emotion" is preferable to the word rage, fine. But emotion can be rage and was. We must recognize our deed and be thankful that America is not a democracy. Consider our Presidential elections if directed by the whims from such good intentions.

I think in the end, Imus failed to recognize the responsibility which free speech demands. All freedoms require individual responsibility. And to that degree, I think we all are guilty. However, I doubt that we will be as correct with ourselves, as we were with Imus.

Vick's Dog Fighting

(September 10, 2007)

AS A THIRTY-EIGHT YEAR OWNER and lover of boxers, I feel a certain and unique anger at what may very well be Michael Vick's lifetime of abuse and cruelty to "man's best friend." I term my anger as "unique" since the muscular appearance of my boxers may also convey a strong and potentially aggressive breed; usually by those unfamiliar with their true loving and tender nature. Since pit bulls present a similar message, I feel "unique" in knowing the truth

In addition to reading about Mr. Vick's admission of guilt, I happened upon an August 22, 1996 Delaware County Daily Times full page article written by a Cindy deProphetis entitled, "Blood Sport. The subtitle, "Trained fighting dogs 'just tearing each other up' in Chester" sadly echoed Vick's costly and illegal hobby.

Ms. deProphetis' writing detailed the cruel and brutal treatment, along with the disregard by law enforcement in 1996 when notified of ongoing and organized dog fights. As one local resident and dog fighting witness stated, "I'd like to see the police enforce the law. They don't do it."

My parents taught, that "there's always an element of good, even in the worst person." Well, the actions of Michael Vick, in addition to being illegal, were brutally inhuman, calloused and sadistic. As a dog owner, I cannot begin to fathom the mind, reason or reward for such depravity. However, with Vick's admission and future sentencing, his promotion of animal gladiators has finally been brought to the public's attention.

This is not just about the Michael Vick case. This is about the preservation of life, the realization that a particular breed is not automatically vicious and that dog fighting is a criminal atmosphere supporting and encouraging other criminal activities. Most importantly, it is about our own morality and integrity in how we approach and deal with barbarity. This needed enforcement and its persistence will serve as our social "yardstick" in judgment of our principled and ethical stability.

We all have the capacity to generate outward disgust and repulsion to a given tragedy. This was amply validated through our 9/11 reactions of anger and shock. However, these emotions dissipate over time and the old adage, "time heals all wounds" comes into play. Care to count how many cars are still flying American flags?

This crusade to protect our four legged buddies will eventually incur a similar re-leveling to our emotions. It's human nature. Pep rallies are not designed to last forever. Obviously, the manner in which approximately three thousand citizens perished on 9/11 will always remain in our hearts and minds. And to a lesser degree, the "sport" of dog fighting is now out in the open. The outcry generated from this despicable action will stay with us if only by the magnitude of its brutality.

Never again will such activities go unreported. What formerly was the case cannot endure. We owe more to our children's playmates and protectors and to those who would unhesitatingly and instinctively give their life for our safety; while asking for so little in return.

We must remember the degree of savagery and suffering inherent with such a vile circus. The second paragraph to that eleven year old article may be uncomfortable to read but very necessary to remember. Ms. deProphetis quotes a lady who witnessed an unspeakable act of cruelty. Consider these words and what may well have been a common occurrence through the intervening years. Ms. deProphetis writes, "I saw a boy cutting a dog's tongue out," she said, not wanting to be fully identified for fear of retribution. "Then he set the dog on fire."

Every time I came in the door from work, my two "ferocious" boxers would come running to greet me as though they hadn't seen me in a year. The warmth and joy they instinctively gave was immeasurable.

While I do think it will somewhat be lessened, I think that the greatest tragedy to Michael Vick's depravity would be for the current outcry to whimper and die. I do not see this happening in total simply because its brutality has been brought out into the open.

All our "best friends" want is love. We have that capacity. More importantly, we have that responsibility. Let us not walk away when such despicable alternatives as torture and brutal beatings change innocence into a bloodthirsty battle for survival!

Why The Media Ignores Ron Paul

(January 21, 2008)

AFTER OVER FORTY YEARS OF being left at the Presidential altar of promises, my impressions of White House integrity hovers between disappointment and embarrassment. Once inaugurated, memory loss seems to be the most common Presidential trait. And, the majority from our current crop of Presidential promisers offer little hope for improved memories and/or promises kept!

My original experience, regarding the integrity of Presidential promises took place during the infamous 1964 contest. During that campaign, President Johnson depicted Barry Goldwater as a war monger. His campaign even went so far as to suggest Goldwater's possible consideration of employing atomic weaponry into our growing Vietnam involvement

Those of my age and older will remember a TV advertisement showing a little girl in a field picking the petals off a daisy as an atomic "mushroom cloud" rose in the background. This pro-Johnson ad turned many voters away from supporting Goldwater.

Also, Johnson promised that if re-elected, he, and I'm paraphrasing, would not send American boys off to fight and die in South East Asia. Johnson beat the "war mongering" Goldwater. Today, we all know the results!

For a young man, of prime draft age, this was not the best introduction to Presidential "take it to the bank" honesty. However, examples of disingenuousness, short memories or just anti-America policies have often comprised the future of our Presidential timber.

Remember back to 1977 as President Carter, a former Naval Academy graduate, selected as his first official act, the granting of amnesty to the many draft evaders living in Canada. Disgraceful as a first Presidential act.

Republican icon, Ronald Reagan's original Presidential campaign promised to dismantle the federal government's unconstitutional Dept. of Education. Once elected, that policy was never mentioned again.

Then there was the time, if I may once again paraphrase, when the first President Bush sternly instructed a gathering of POW/MIA families to, more or less, sit down and shut up!

How about the campaign promises of Bill Clinton to dedicate, as a major administration priority, a full and complete accounting of our Vietnam POW/MIAs prior to any normalization with Vietnam? Another instance of a short memory after winning the White House.

Then the most recent Bush pledged during his first campaign that if elected, his administration would "not nation build"! Of course the tragic events of 9/11 offered some wiggle room but then again, in one of his first speeches to the Nation after that tragedy, he promised that this attack "would not change America." His Patriot Act stands as a sad and unconstitutional contradiction.

As I now confront another parade of Presidential aspirants who once again bellow the ageless promise of change, I fully expect that what is said on the campaign trail will have little to do with the finished product. That is, except for one candidate with a rare but lengthy paper trail of honesty and integrity. His value to our Nation has not only been indisputably recorded by his performance in Congress but evidently is validated by the media's intentional discrediting and minimizing amount of coverage. Consider the credentials of Ron Paul.

As a Vietnam veteran, I fully agree with his Constitutional belief that only Congress has the authority to declare war. Ironically, America also lacks a military victory for as long as this requirement has been ignored.

Rep. Paul believes so-called free trade treaties and entangling global alliances such as NAFTA, GATT, CAFTA and the WTO threaten our country's independent sovereignty and strength. Makes sense when comparing our current industrial and manufacturing output verses pre-NAFTA levels!

Ron Paul supports individual property rights against the special interest manipulations of Eminent Domain claims. He also believes a strict enforcement of property rights corrects environmental injustices. He is against the government's desire of collecting and storing the data of citizens' personal matters. He is against the taxing of the "tip" income from those in the service industry and defends the freedom of American families to home school their children. He is also against the Dept. of Education and would strive to abolish it. Also, in a free society, he believes that each citizen must maintain the right to keep and bear arms. Finally, a secure border is a must since a nation without a border is not a nation.

An interesting side note about a candidate which few Americans know about. His campaign contributions from members of the military are the most of any in the race!

In Congress, he has never voted for a tax increase, an unbalanced budget nor has he ever taken a government paid junket during his twenty years of service. He is also a very rare "public servant" for refusing to participate in the lucrative congressional pension program!

This voting record and his policy positions reflect why Ron Paul's campaign remains in the media's shadows. Still, his Constitutional beliefs and positions are being heard as internet popularity and usage explodes.

Today, brazen promises of additional governmental entitlements and various subsidies seem as the norm for political platforms while candidates speaking the hard truth are generally ignored by media outlets. Such voter enticement amounts to the corruption of a free society through the spirit of the vote.

In closing, our media commits a disservice to our citizens by limiting its coverage to "the leading vote getters" of the major parties. All should be given equal opportunity to voice their candidacy, not just those promising handouts. This selective airing, by our nation's media, features a manipulative tool for maintaining this questionable level of integrity with our leaders today. It is a process which we can ill afford.

Presidential Candidates' Hot Air

(March 26, 2008)

THE RECENT TELEVISED PRESIDENTIAL DEBATES provide a glimpse into just how controlled and limited the age of information has become, specifically by revealing the ease of manipulating public thought and concern. As such, one must wonder whether an improvement in leadership is still a viable goal!

This mental persuasion centers upon the rehashing of well worn "political footballs" while more pressing and even threatening topics are never mentioned.

What more can be said of the financially troubled Social Security system when illegal immigrants are allowed to partake? How much more debate or money will it require to correct the failure of public education? And at what point do we as patriotic Americans demand that our Country be secure? When will the candidates understand that fences are not the answer? Just ask any dog owner!

Do we really have faith in a bumbling federal authority to administer health care for all Americans? Other than collecting taxes, what does Washington do efficiently? If the "most powerful military in the world" cannot win a war in the last 60 some years, just how in hell can we expect proper medical care?

Then there's always the war issue itself. This level of concern should have been addressed prior to our invading Iraq. America is setting a not so honorable pattern of leaving the kitchen when it gets too hot.

These are promoted as the issues of the day. Need I also mention that through all these debates, "change" is once again being promised to the voters? This may be the most insulting, yet alluring, of all public expectations. How many were aware of a 1994 Philadelphia Inquirer headline, "'Change,' the 92 buzzword, is heard louder in '94." This come on just seems to rejuvenate itself every other year.

Candidates running for office have promised "change" ever since the second political campaign. For the most part, the only "change" to occur has been in the negative direction. And that is the fascination to the word. Everyone expects change to be beneficial. Just as there are two sides to a coin, "change" is two-sided as well!

The issues mention above, such as Social Security and health care, have and would be federally created. More importantly, they are creations outside of our Constitutional parameters. However, they all mesmerize and command attention. The grittier or more threatening issues are intentionally scratched from the arena of debate, as was exemplified just recently.

A couple of weeks ago, I was curious as to the subjects discussed during the Democratic debate in Texas. Being a "border state," citizens in the Lone Star State are heavily inundated from this continuing Mexican invasion. While the pluses and minuses of building a fence were discussed, it became obvious that questions from the audience were not to be.

Given the fact that just a year ago, Texas Governor Perry denied that there were plans for what is now called a "NAFTA Superhighway, the moderators scripted their questioning in such a manner to avoid any such reference. Obviously, a three football field highway width garners a high amount of interest to not only Texans but to all associated citizens in the intended states where this behemoth will be built. Legislators in some of those effected states are already introducing bills which will ban such an invasive project. This is only one example to the list of issues that are being conveniently avoided by both parties.

As to the debates themselves, it appears that they also provided a method for which the more qualified candidates from both parties were eliminated. If judged solely upon the qualification of experience, how can U.S. Sens. Hillary Clinton or Barack Obama compare to Sens. Christopher Dodd, Joseph Biden or New Mexico Gov. Bill Richardson? On the Republican side, while McCain's service in the Senate is extensive, he somehow outlasted other candidates who, on the important issue of immigration, were in tune with the public's recent outcry. His success would appear as "Rocky" like, if not media pre-ordained.

Candidates aside, the issues being ignored are relevant to our present and future generations. As we all are well aware, America has become a "debtor nation." Why then do we continue to spend over $20 billion per year in foreign aid? Is America's expensive membership in the United Nations an asset or a liability? Does it make sense to provide Social Security to illegals who have returned to Mexico?

And what of this North American Union plan to merge Mexico, the United States and Canada? Combine this little known fact with the previously mention NAFTA Superhighway providing its economic lifeline! Given the millions of jobs lost since NAFTA's creation, why not withdraw from this "sucking sound" of insanity?

The debate's refrain for hashing out decade-old issues may well serve as an omen to our long expected promise for "change." Could there be a hidden purpose for not discussing these more pressing issues and ominous threats? If so, these omissions may actually present a more accurate telling as to the coming winds of change.

Rothkopf's 'Superclass' Editorial

(June 11, 2008)

TWO FACTS CAN BE LEARNED from the highly informative, yet threatening editorial entitled, "They're Global Citizens. They're Hugely Rich. And They Pull the Strings," appearing in the Washington Post on May 4th.

One, the "conspiracy theory" is now an admitted fact, and second, it apparently has experienced an unexpected degree of success; so much so that the author, David Rothkopf, conducts his boasting in a public venue.

The opening of Mr. Rothkopf's article offensively declares that, "We didn't elect them. We can't throw them out. And they're getting more powerful every day. Call them the superclass."

Mr. Rothkopf brags about an unidentified organization, numbering approximately 6000 members, which maintains such a global influence as being able to employ what the writer describes as a "convening power;" one which can "get the big boys of Wall Street and world financial capitals into a room or on a conference call to collaborate on solving a problem" without the inconsequential limits of national governments.

This, along with a "power and ability to regularly influence millions of lives across international borders," which in reality reduces or even eliminates the effectiveness of national identity or sovereignty, sadly constitutes what the conspiracy theorists have been warning about as a coming "world order!"

Practically all fields of endeavor are credited with having leading members from this "superclass." Areas such as investment, corporate executives, members of banking's top echelon, media bigwigs, political heads of state, general grade military officers, leading members of the scientific community and religious leaders present a blanket of control worthy of more than just the public's deep concern and curiosity. This poses a "clear and present danger" at the most heinous level—especially so when this "superclass" admits the inclusion of the "heads of terrorist and criminal organizations!"

This in-place structure, designed for bringing about a global order must have as its target our inalienable rights, our Constitutional rule of law along with our American sovereignty. Replacing such blessings of liberty and opportunity will be the whimsical nature of an unsavory internationalist gang devoid of any loyalties other than profit. A rather insecure forecast at best.

Now consider our current societal trends and mindsets which have already been significantly altered through a gradual inch by inch process. Sadly, Americans have now grown accustomed to being financially dependent upon the decisions from a far away international conglomerate without any allegiance to our people or our Nation. This international inching process can be best realized in the three letters spelling gas. No wonder Mr. Rothkopf feels comfortable with his boastful anticipation for a world controlled by a "superclass."

When taking account of American resolve to defend what is precious and dear, our disunity becomes a glaring weakness. Glaring to such an extent that it may have been a useful tool employed by these greedy and unscrupulous captains of intrigue. The element of cohesiveness, which can be attributable to our WWII success, has long since evaporated. I doubt that this unbelievable global scheme could even have been seriously deliberated without the added assurance of a plan to "divide and conquer."

In concert with our many societal divisions, also consider the many societal changes, which if judged objectively, amount to a devaluing of respect, authority and traditional values.

Quite possibly, our transformational slide could very well have begun on the day when our President was assassinated in Dallas. Nothing would ever be taken for granted again. For over fifty years, a comparing of the standards and traditions before that fateful day to our current permissive attitudes shows a consistent downward spiral, easily validated through newspaper headlines and every citizen's personal experience.

The cornerstone to any successful society is the family unit. Judge for yourself the present state of single parent households. Then take a hard look at the educational standards at which our children become enlightened. And lastly, what does the future hold for current and future generations when corporate greed removes any possibility for gainful employment.

This is not the America which my generation experienced! In contrast to the current political race for the Presidency, and particularly with the voter's fascination with the word "change," America in the last half century, has been negatively and consistently assaulted by "change." Even Mr. Rothkopf's closing included an ominous prediction concerning that magic word. To quote, "'change' isn't just a slogan in this year's campaign. It's a reality that will redefine the landscape of power worldwide for U.S. presidents of the future."

In the final analysis, two steps are required for combating this insidious assault, First, contrary to Mr. Rothkopf's intent due to his own membership, the identity of that secretive organization is The Council on Foreign Relations, located in New York City and Washington, D.C. As an example of its effectiveness, an average of 400 to 500 members are interspersed throughout our Federal government.

Secondly, we must temper any urge for anger, and instead, regard these arrogant and rare admissions as a timely and useful warning. For if we continue to turn our heads or ridicule the notion of a conspiracy, then Mr. Rothkopf's un-American predictions for our future will be realized, too late!

Palin Offers 'Can-Do' Spirit

(October 9, 2008)

IF THE SELECTION OF SARAH Palin was indeed a welcomed alternative producing a reinvigorating atmosphere to the Republican ticket and the Presidential elections in general, why then is there this media upheaval bordering, in some cases, upon disgust?

Could it be as simple as the media's injured vanity since McCain and his staff were able to keep her selection secret? Since the magnitude of a lead story about an unknown would have been a media blockbuster, being kept in the dark could be unforgivable.

Unfortunately, I don't think it to be that simple!

No, this secretive political coup has come to signify more than a surprising Vice Presidential choice. While it is true that Gov. Palin's selection has almost instantly reenergized the electorate with both interest and a thought that honest government can be achieved, our expensive Federal bureaucracy is reeling with disbelief and shock at the probability for real change.

Based upon her record as the Governor of Alaska, the possibilities from an unpredictable second in command is unthinkable. Thus, amassing an Alaskan bound investigative horde was born out of self preservation. While its ensuing revelations seem insignificant by comparison, the searches continue.

Gov. Palin represents a bit more than a possible shaking up of political shenanigans. Her presence embodies Americanism, a return to a "can do" belief in one's ability and determination. Her enthusiastic and direct approach brings fresh air to this fog of futility; one which has elevated the "welfare state" into unbridled prominence.

This rekindled American spirit represents a direct threat to an emerging dynamic born out of guilt for America's success.

This mental paralysis has taken hold of our youngest voting generation for too long. The McCain ticket, with emphasis upon Palin's history of disrupting the status quo, presents at least an untimely setback to the required nurturing of this un-American and anti capitalistic mindset. Electing Obama will not only serve this interest but will actually strengthen its process. The protection for this ongoing ideological shift, along with the added plum of possibly realizing a democratically controlled Federal government, not only provides a sufficient motive but also outweighs any hesitation to this first ever no-holds-barred despicable campaign agenda.

In concert with the ongoing treason to our economy, continuing this changing approach to freedom, opportunity and limited government will also require the future devaluation of respectful campaign decorum whenever needed. No longer will the families of candidates receive a "Chelsea Clinton pass."

Returning to that investigative invasion of Alaska, an over publicized question detailing the firing of a highly placed State official seems to be heading a short list of possible "scandals."

In a shameful attempt to garner the public's ire, media pundits label this controversy as "Troopergate." Makes one wonder if the "gate" identity will ever escape from journalistic abuse.

Another media ruse is the mundane question of whether Gov. Palin was for "the bridge to nowhere" before she was against it.

More importantly, she happens to have a seventeen year old pregnant daughter who has yet to walk down the aisle. Ironically, the majority of Americans regard these findings as insultingly unfair and especially so when featuring personal and/or family affairs.

Finally, futility and desperation shines through the questioning of her foreign affairs expertise as her experience is limited to the State level.

This question also insults when considering the backgrounds of recent Presidents. Carter, Reagan, Clinton and Bush all exemplified the smooth transition from State to Federal authority.

A very disturbing fact, which largely went unreported by our Nation's media, has surfaced with regards to the Obama candidacy. Obviously, but judge for yourself, the over hyped Palin controversies pale by comparison.

It has been reported by the New York Post that while on his recent overseas tour, Sen. Obama inappropriately suggested to the Iraqi Foreign

Minister, Hoshyar Zebari, to delay an agreement on a draw down of the American military presence until after the next administration takes office.

I mention this incredulous action by Obama as an unbiased presentation of a factual event which hopefully creates a pause against the media hype to glorify Obama.

The degree of coverage assigned to inconsequential Alaskan dirt digging verses an indifference to Obama's sad and possibly illegal request of Iraq's Foreign Minister tells it all!

In today's world, Americans are putting their lives on the line once again. Strong leadership counts! Add experience and it becomes a no-brainer. My generation had to deal with inept leadership and failed policies from supposedly "the best and the brightest!"

Today's military does not need a replay of a McNamara two-step. Voting for a President who would delay the return of service men and women exemplifies that ballroom dancing from years past!

Changing Constitutional Interpretations

(December 4, 2008)

ON THANKSGIVING, ONE OF MY dinner guests was a young mother chasing a college degree. Having brought her "history" book along with her eight month old son, I invaded her study time as my curiosity demanded that I check out what I've suspected for a while.

Her textbook entitled, "We The People: An Introduction to American Politics," soon validated my suspicions on just one page. The subject matter, "presidential power," detailed three types of power available along with an explanation of the term "executive order."

Now before relating what I read, I fully realize that the Constitution's strict limits have long since become blurred through endless interpretations. These illegalities have become so common place that they now are enshrined as subject matter for our young. Teaching governmental abuse as how proper government operates gives little chance for good citizenship and less chance for realizing when one's rights are being abused.

This new version of "American politics" presents the reader with an explanation of an "executive order" on page 489. It teaches that such an order is "a rule or regulation issued by the President that has the effect and formal status of legislation."

Granted, this illegal practice has continued throughout the 20th century. However, that does not legalize a Constitutional wrong.

Our Constitution clearly states that Congress is the branch in which law making authority rests. Teaching that a "Presidential executive order" carries the same effectiveness as Congressional legislation is simply incorrect and in doing so commits a disservice to the students by fracturing the quality of American governmental understanding. It also devalues the subsequent quality of American citizenship and in the end, promotes additional abuse.

Further, this "must read" volume details three individual powers available to the President. The first, "expressed powers," as its definition explains, "Specific powers granted by the Constitution to Congress (Art I Sect. 8) and to the President (Art II)," is the only recognized and legitimate authority and the only one of the three to be referenced by the Constitution.

By explaining the next two "powers," education starts to slide down a slippery hallucinogenic slope. The second is the "delegated power." Its definition is as follows, "constitutional powers that are assigned to one governmental agency but that are exercised by another agency with the express permission of the first." Are you kiddin me? Is that a grab bag of nothing or what? When the Constitution assigns authority, that is where that authority lies. It cannot be traded, reassigned or placed in a governmental lottery. Changes to the Constitution can only be attempted through the amendment process.

The final "power" gets even better. "Inherent powers" are defined as, "powers claimed by a President that are not expressed in the Constitution, but are inferred from it." And, this is what is being taught in colleges today!

The word "infer" is without legal standing since it is defined as "to imply, hint." Certainly not the caliber of Constitutional tenets.

Whether it be regarded as mistruths, misinformation or just outright lies, this is the grist from where so many misconceptions originate. Is there any wonder as to the source of America being considered a democracy? The same holds true about "the separation of church and state" myth.

For me, that single textbook page answered many questions and quelled many more suspicions. For one thing, where is the authorization for the Federal Government's Public Education Department? There is none so it's illegal! Since this is an illegal enterprise, is it so surprising that the ultimate effort or purpose is to confuse and mislead? Certainly, one cannot expect to learn of the proper role of Constitutional government by a federal entity which, if truth be known, lacks any legal standing! The Department of Education is not meant to educate, nor is it meant to tattle on themselves. It's only function seems to limit and control public knowledge.

Finally, our Forefathers considered an education incomplete if ample time was not devoted to the teachings of the Christian religion. General religious activity or expression was termed unconstitutional in a 1947 Supreme Court ruling. Amazingly, from our founding period to that date, such freedoms were Constitutional. Obviously the Constitution hasn't changed but modern day interpretations certainly have! The misinformation and unfounded beliefs currently being circulated not only offer credence to these changing interpretations but also should enhance our concerns for the Constitution's future.

Understanding Our Constitutional Rights

(January 23, 2009)

A NEWS ITEM OF NATIONAL consequence, "Supreme Court: Evidence in despite mistakes," appeared locally on January 15th, sending chills from its ominous police state preference verses proper Constitutional conduct.

The brief article reported that "The justices split 5-4 along ideological lines to apply new limits to the court's so-called exclusionary rule, which generally requires evidence to be suppressed if it results from a violation of a suspect's Fourth Amendment right to be free from unreasonable searches or seizure."

The Court's finding that "evidence obtained after illegal searches and arrests based on simple police mistakes may be used to prosecute criminal defendants." This boggles the mind since this finding is directly contrary to the law of the land.

Though the Court acknowledged that the arrest violated the suspect's Constitutional rights, since it was conducted upon the mistaken belief that there was a warrant for his arrest already in existence, "the conservative majority . . . upheld his conviction on federal drug and gun charges."

Causing immediate concern was the ruling being based "along ideological lines!" Are you kiddin me? The function of the Supreme Court is to uphold, defend and interpret the original meanings to our Constitution! Ideologies of any stripe must be left at the door.

Are we supposed to believe that the suspect in question, one Bennie Dean Herring was deprived of his inalienable Fourth Amendment rights simply based upon the personal ideologies of five robed justices? Wrong!

One should read our Fourth Amendment to determine the degree of injustice, which this decision required. It states, "The right of the people to be secure in their persons, houses, papers and effects, against unreasonable searches and seizures, shall not be violated, and no warrants shall issue, but upon probable cause, supported by oath or affirmation, and particularly describing the place to be searched, and the persons or things to be seized."

Since there wasn't an existing warrant, the initial stop itself was illegal since "probable cause" was never verified or even offered in pursuant to a search warrant. Therefore, the subsequent evidence seized was illegally obtained. How five Supreme Court justices could admit that the arrest (not to mention the original stop) "violated his Constitutional rights" yet still managed to uphold his conviction is a travesty of justice!

Now given the public sentiment generated from years of watching the guilty avoid prosecution on the televised series Law and Order, the temptation may be great to turn the other way and feel that even though the suspect's rights were violated, he was never the less guilty. Wrong!

This rationalizing reminds me of those who believe that since they have nothing to hide, "what's wrong with the police searching my house?"

In an orderly and free society, rules must be obeyed. That pertains to both citizens and to every level of authority. Our Bill of Rights is solely meant to limit our Federal authority. However, since every State entering the Union had to be fashioned upon a similar Republican form of government, just about every inalienable right listed in our Bill of Rights can be found in the Constitutions of every State.

The Declaration of Rights, found in Article I of the Constitution of the Commonwealth of Pennsylvania, adheres to such conformity with its Section 8 subject of "Security from Searches and Seizures."

The bottom line to this is the judicial system's growing usurpation of Congress's legislative role. Since this flawed decision, law enforcement agencies around the Country have been given a green light for such unprecedented conduct. Sad to say, this abhorrent ruling is the latest to a long judicial list of curtailing individual rights through the misinterpretation of our Constitution. The ease in which these injustices are passed come as the direct result from a quiet and passive citizenry.

Not only have our citizens become indifferent to judicial usurpations, they are often encouraged by misinformation and/or emotion. Consider what has resulted over the years from another incorrect Supreme Court interpretation in which the 1947 Everson v. Board of Education ruling stated, "The First Amendment has erected a wall between church and state." Now, I'm not a legal scholar! Show me the words to that effect in our First Amendment since I can't find them!

There is little doubt as to the element of emotions having encouraged the identical illegal search and seizure tactics associated with our DUI roadblocks. Authority cannot legally stop law abiding citizens without either observing probable cause or by obtaining a warrant based upon probable cause. However, judicial rulings condone this Constitutional exception by citing the increase safety it provides to society. Again, while good intentioned, these findings are wrong!

There exists a delicate balance within the framework of a free society. The expectation for individual responsibility works hand in hand with the limitations placed upon authority at all levels. Currently, it seems that individual need has become too burdensome while authority expands.

Finally, in Pennsylvania's Constitution, Section 2 states, "All power is inherent in the people." Maybe, instead of listening to Law and Order complain about the "technicalities" of individual rights, we should begin to understand our rights, proper judicial authority and the limitations which define our Constitutional Republic. That is, while we are still allowed to.

Putting Trust In 'Original Intent'

(March 7, 2009)

THERE IS NO DOUBT THAT the visions of our Forefathers are being drastically revised, ignored, criticized or just plain defied. The latest piece of evidence to this ongoing effort was offered from a Los Angeles Times article which appeared in my local Florida newspaper on February 24th under the heading of, "Court to decide church-state issue."

Within the opening paragraph, it was reported that, "The Supreme Court agreed Monday to decide whether a cross can stand in a national park in California to honor fallen soldiers."

This article further comments upon the close division between the Supreme Court justices as to whether "religious symbols, such as the Ten Commandments or a depiction of Christ's birth, can be displayed on public property." As to be expected, this is just the latest assault upon our Christian-Judeo heritage by that infamous guardian of our Constitution, the American Civil Liberties Union. This particular case resulted from a governmental denial to "a request to have a Buddhist shrine erected near the cross."

While I'm fully aware that our nation's economic downturn garners most of our attention, we must also be jealously aware and protective of what distinguishes America from the rest of the world. As this difference continues to be questioned, revised or eliminated, it is this American individualism which should be most highly prized and defended.

While the particulars of this future Supreme Court case will center around religious symbolism, the entire "church-state" debate originated out of thin air.

To be an issue necessitating Supreme Court judgment, this argument must have Constitutional grounding. It doesn't! The bogus issue of "a

140

separation of church and state" was taken out of context from a letter in which Thomas Jefferson wrote to the Danbury (Conn.) Baptists on January 1ˢᵗ, 1801.

What eventually provided the legal impetus, which has produced our current misunderstanding to this issue, began in that same court with their 1947 Everson ruling. The only previous Supreme Court reference to Jefferson's 1801 letter was recorded in a Supreme Court judgment in the 1878 Reynolds v. United States case. And, in that 1878 case, Jefferson's entire letter was published!

In an extremely well defined, documented and infinitely researched work entitled "Original Intent"—'the Courts, the Constitution, and Religion,' David Barton writes, "Jefferson believed" as is well documented from his personal writings, "that God, not government, was the Author and Source of our rights and that government, therefore, was prevented from interference with those rights." Or in Jefferson's own words, "And can the liberties of a nation be thought secure if we have lost the only firm basis, a conviction in the minds of the people that these liberties are the gift of God? That they are not to be violated but with his Wrath?"

Considering this brief excerpt from our Forefather's beliefs and intentions, can any logical thinking person sit still while nine black robed justices waste time pondering upon a non issue? How do they walk up those front steps leading to their courtroom while seeing Moses holding the Ten Commandments inscribed in the stone atop of their building? Even the two oak doors leading into the courtroom contain the Ten Commandments! Also, the wall behind where the justices sit displays Moses and the Ten Commandments. I fail to see this "separation" even in the room where such trivial pursuits of "separation" are theorized.

In our "land of the free," what sense or purpose do these illegal rulings serve? This seems to be an inherent contradiction to the meaning of our inalienable rights.

It's only been a little more than two centuries since our Forefathers sacrificed so that we may live in freedom. Yet, through the interpretations and gradual encroachments from our high browed revisionist sect, (a politically correct term describing any believer of anti American doctrines), we have succumbed to their never ending chant that our Constitution is a "living" document. If this were true it would be akin to saying that our system of law is without the rigidity of standards.

Having just read a very interesting and profoundly logical assessment of our growing and recklessly uncontrolled Supreme Court, written by Edwin Vieira J., a lawyer who successfully championed three cases at that level, he dismisses the usual legal jargon as he plainly explains that, "'original intent' was then and remains today the one and only practical and legitimate means for interpreting the Constitution."

As a grateful American, I would rather put my trust and belief in that "original intent" forged and finely honed by struggle and sacrifice.

Sen. McCarthy Needed
In Socialist Times

(May 27, 2009)

AFTER FINISHING M. STANTON EVANS' voluminous 600 page work entitled Blacklisted By History, I began to understand the why's and wherefores to all this anti-American sentiment which seems to permeate the majority of generations following mine.

For the longest time, I felt reasonably sure that its roots were nurtured during those violent years of Vietnam protests. While this obviously sped the process, the origins began long before the slogan "hell no, I won't go" became fashionable.

Mr. Evans' book provides a detailed accounting of the trials and tribulations of one Sen. Joe McCarthy.

First, understand that from never-ending accounts, which negatively portrayed Sen. McCarthy, his image of being a "demagogue, a bully, and a liar" remains firmly fixed within the American conscience. Nothing could be further from the truth! Our media victimizes its hallowed ground of truth and honesty when accounts continue to draw upon this false impression. Today however, "his name remains synonymous with witch hunts."

M. Stanton Evans spent "six years of intensive research" which included "never before-published government records and FBI files, as well as recent research gleaned from Soviet archives and intercepted transmissions between Moscow spymasters and their agents in the United States."

Through its shocking content, Mr. Evans "presents irrefutable evidence of a relentless Communist drive to penetrate our government, influence its policies, and steal its secrets." Most unbelievable is Mr. Evans' depiction "that U.S. officials supposedly guarding against this danger not only let it happen but actively covered up the penetration."

I mention Mr. Evans' highly documented work to illustrate and connect what is currently taking place in today's society. I am certain that this anti-American attitude is not just a figment of my imagination since many have mentioned noticing this phenomenon during casual conversations.

In addition to this rising discontent, many societal divisions which have appeared since Vietnam, are kept aflame through an incendiary method of reporting. Diversity, racism, class envy/jealousy are just a few which spew suspicion, hatred and isolation. As our United States continues to be splintered and fractionalized, is it such a far reach to connect the dots back to what Sen. McCarthy tried to uncover? I think not!

Approximately ten years elapsed from the end of the "McCarthy Era" till the nationwide protests against Vietnam. This effort was not only massive in size, but well coordinated from its beginning. Seeds of discontent had to be planted in young minds many years prior in order to amass such a loud echo of uniformed protests.

Prior to those turbulent years, I am aware of only one entity which embraced such an anti-American platform. That being the Communist Party USA, or CPUSA. Since their presence was in all fifty States, their structure provided an ability and motive to spread anti-American venom while coordinating future protests nation wide.

One result from the McCarthy investigations was the realization that government employment brought the possibility for this type of scrutiny in the future. This sense of vulnerability caused many to scurry into the more secured private sector. Academia also offered unchallenged respect.

Some may challenge my connecting of dots but I witnessed first hand the transformation from a peaceful, proud and harmonious society into one of violent confrontations bordering upon anarchy in a very short time span. This sharp and immediate contrast, from congenial order to sometimes violent protest, had to enjoy an incubation period which also provided the necessary time for planning such a large scale undertaking.

My critics will point to the Vietnam War as an ignition point but I believe that it provided not only an excuse but an opportunity to begin the disruption our cohesive society.

In the end, one question begs answering. Why did two Presidents, one from each party, deem it necessary to not only question but to fiercely hamper and/or derail McCarthy's investigations, even to the point of slandering his personal reputation? Was not his purpose, to rid Communists and Soviet agents from within our Federal government, a worthwhile endeavor? After all, our Country was in the Cold War against the very enemy for which those secret agents served!

There is no mistaking the growing anti-American sentiment in this country. Some may point to coincidence, happenstance or to a natural progression. However, shedding our cloaks of freedom and inalienable rights for this growing cloud of socialistic governance is in direct opposition to a natural order. Therefore, this suicidal transition has to be incited.

It was this influence that Sen. McCarthy tried to uncover. He failed and we are now faced with today's army of socialistic purveyors who have matriculated into society's many influential and illuminated positions of authority.

Instead of Joe DiMaggio, the song should say, "where have you gone Joe McCarthy, our nation needs you . . ."

Remember Cost of Freedom

(May 31, 2010)

ANOTHER MEMORIAL DAY IS QUICKLY approaching. As a veteran of Vietnam, I have much to remember, much to give thanks for and much to live up to. While our veteran history began at Concord and Lexington in 1775, pages continue to be written today in Iraq and Afghanistan.

Given our history of service and sacrifice, it seems a bit incongruous when considering the trespasses and violations which have occurred to our Constitution and way of life. Especially so when realizing the current amount of veterans who have previously protected and defended our Constitution.

Today, our public officials flaunt their obnoxious airs with an equal amount of distain for the average voter. Asked if the recent healthcare legislation was Constitutional, Pelosi replied, "are you kiddin, are you kiddin?" Sadly, not one person felt the need to say, "No, we are not kiddin!"

Pelosi's attitude is prevalent today on both sides of the aisle. Sadly, this reflects back upon us all. Either by complicity or apathy, we the voters are responsible for the fall of the rigid standards set forth by our Forefathers. Up until now, our silence has been their encouragement.

So on this day of remembrance to the loyalty, service and sacrifice of our Nation's brothers and sisters, it seems fitting to quote a few words spoken at our Nation's most costly battlefield. The closing words of Lincoln's Gettysburg Address should reacquaint Americans with the duties required by freedom.

President Lincoln stated in closing, "That from these honored dead we take increased devotion to that cause for which they gave the last full measure of devotion; that we here highly resolve that these dead shall not have died in vain; that this nation under God shall have a new birth of freedom; and that government of the people, by the people, for the people, shall not perish from the earth." This was said in 1863.

After close to a hundred and fifty years after his Address, we all must consider the amount of freedom which has been lost through the tyranny of legislative usurpation.

Far from the force of war, generations of today seem content to "go along to get along," or to "not rock the boat." This is abhorrent when compared with our American heritage.

To all my fellow veterans who swore fidelity to the Constitution, I say "enough is enough." Our Country has been steered off course. It is up to us, the proven, to right its way. Being an American has always been and still is a special title. However, it also demands a responsible guardianship so that succeeding generations will have the same opportunities.

On this day of special remembrance to devotion and sacrifice, we should also take a moment to rededicate ourselves to the allegiance which we once swore. We must protect and defend our Country, not with weapons but with peaceful unity of purpose. For what we swore to in our youth still is in play. It still counts for as long as we live.

On this Memorial Day, maybe we all should make it a point to listen to Kate Smith singing "God Bless America." Follow those inspiring words and our course will be obvious. God Bless our veterans, past and present and our Country.

Constitutional Abuse

(August 29, 2010)

THIS INCESSANT DRUMBEAT, TESTING NOT just the will and knowledge of our people but also probing for a weakness in our Constitutional guarantees is really getting old.

In all likelihood, a successful usurpation of our Constitutional rights continues to be thwarted by the word "inalienable." Its definition resembles a traffic light stuck on red to those who would whimsically revise our blessings from birth.

Thomas Jefferson said it best in our Declaration of Independence when laying the foundation to our freedom with the words, "endowed by their Creator" (for emphasis, Jefferson's use of a capital "C"), "with certain inalienable rights . . ." This distinction acknowledges that our individual rights, of which our second Amendment is certainly one, are rights inherited at birth from our "Creator." As such, they are above the corruptive machinery which is so characteristic of big government. Or as Jefferson described, "the mischief of man." This is the lesson to be studied by those so intent upon altering and ultimately erasing our blessings of freedom.

Apparently, from reading the website version of the Delco Times (Pa.), a State Congressman by the name of Bryan Lentz, follows such an unconstitutional path with his proposed House Bill 2536. While based upon that insidious justification of "good intentions," it never-the-less is just part of a piecemeal attack designed to culminate with the eventual elimination of our Second amendment rights. So, I feel compelled to add my two cents from far away Florida since I too experienced this unconstitutional abridgement of my rights as a long time resident of Delco. (Delaware County, Pa.)

After carrying a duly licensed weapons carry permit for five years, I was notified that a renewal application was required. To make a long story short, I was denied my renewal based upon a conviction for "drag racing" in 1968. From April 1995 till April 3, 2000, I was legally licensed to carry a firearm.

Following my denial challenge in Harrisburg, the Pennsylvania State Police mailed a letter dated July 13, 2000, that stated and I quote, "the decision to deny your request is upheld based upon your conviction in 1968 to VC1041, Drag Racing, defined as a misdemeanor offense, and punishable by a maximum term of imprisonment of three years." Insultingly, the following sentence was underlined. It informed me that, "Please be advised that regardless of any penalty that you may have received, this decision is based on the maximum penalty you could have received for this offense(s)."

Now, in 2010, all I have to say about this ruling is, "Are you kiddin' me?" Number one, traffic violations incurring "points" start reducing after one year. Secondly, insurance rates return to normal amounts after five years. Finally, traffic violations are to be expunged from one's record after seven years. This denial occurred THIRTY-TWO years after the violation. In addition, since when is a denial to an inalienable right based not upon punishment but what could have been the punishment?

Ten years have passed since my challenge in Harrisburg. I am well into my sixties with only one speeding ticket to my name during that span of time. Prior to my drag racing escapade, I was issued and was qualified with weapons during my two years as a Military Policeman in the US Army.

Apparently, Rep. Lentz places higher value upon the voter appeal aspect verses Constitutional guarantees when voicing those anti-gun/anti-carry words. The Times article informed its readers that "Pennsylvania residents who are not eligible for a permit to carry a concealed weapon" would be prevented "from using a permit issued by another state, while they are in Pennsylvania.", if in fact, Rep. Lentz's bill is passed. Instead of viewing it as a threat, could it be a citizen's legal option to an abusive law?

I think that the Congressman from Swarthmore ought to concern himself more with the out of control State budget than his targeting of law abiding citizens who seek self protection.

One other suggestion if I may. Barring a lawful citizen from exercising his or her inalienable right of self protection, based upon a "could of," is a crime far worse than the misdemeanor which was originally cited.

Finally, it remains our Constitutional duty as law abiding American citizens to resist illegal and/or immoral laws such as House Bill 2536. Maybe Rep. Lentz should familiarize himself with the proper exercise of authority rather than pandering to the vocal few. Just another suggestion from far away.

Obama's Marxist Agenda Must End

(October 28, 2010)

THIS CURRENT ELECTION SEASON IS a public showcase filled with examples of just how false and hollow our leadership has become. Not one candidate for re-election is running on his or her voting record. This acid test more than validates reasons for discontinuing President Barack Obama's Marxist agenda.

While every election bears consequence, our mid-term choices will either save or doom our nation's future. If this seems to be an over estimation, just consider what has taken place during the past 20-plus months. The resulting policies are of such magnitude that many view this November without any Democrat or Republican considerations. These long-standing ideologies and/or preferences have fallen by the wayside since it has become obvious that the voice of the people has been ignored time after time. Our government now operates under the assumption that it knows better than the American public.

Many of today's Democrats and Republicans feel at best, un-represented and at worse, betrayed from these ears of stone. As each humiliation mounts, the latest as Congress adjourns without any thought to passing next year's budget or tackling the 2011 federal tax rates, members of both parties are beginning to find common ground under the tea party banner.

As re-election probabilities continue to dwindle, many have resorted to personal attack verses an intelligent explanation of past and present policies.

Many candidates, who have aligned themselves with the Obama doctrines rather than hearing the demands from their constituents, now face an unwanted but an unavoidable accounting from their employers.

151

Arrogance and power are the germs producing many of the ills emanating from Washington today. The result, which is quickly unifying many Americans is the unmistakable residue from being insulted. This does not set too well with the temperament of the average American.

Too many issues are geared upon such blatant affronts. After passing healthcare, against the will of the majority of Americans, we are now being told that in order to insure those mystical 30 million uninsured, rates will have to increase. In other words, "Who didn't know that?"

Along with this insulting but unifying healthcare issue, another example of an unresponsive and belligerent government takes place within the confines of Arizona. By recalling the unity following 9/11, when all Americans became proud and defiant New Yorkers, in similar reactive support, we are all becoming proud and defiant Arizonians.

If there is a lesson to be learned from 9/11, Washington has skipped the class. Instead, they rely upon the authority of their office. They will once again force their authority upon the American public. Or so they intend. This "in your face" authority is not American and will not be tolerated. Again, another lesson to be learned which government, so far, has ignored.

In a very real sense, the ambitions of Obama, along with the resulting one-party dominance, ushered in a mindset which felt confident to ignore any constitutional limitation upon its rule. The one mistake amid this continuous power grab was an underestimating of the American people. Our disunity and our constitutional irreverence were foolishly assumed. However, both were strengthened through Obama's overreaching authority.

Public defiance against illegal policies are precisely constitutional and has left the power brokers stunned and for once, speechless.

Their arsenal is limited to the personal attacks of past, present and inconsequential actions. Those that have ruled with zestful public insolence are now reduced to the level of tabloid accusations for one simple reason. Their voting records are the grist attributing to the public's anger. As they continue down the path of personal attacks against their opponents, they only validate the fact that passing legislation against public opinion comes with a price.

For once, the electorate is witnessing the inter-workings of what has appropriately been termed "the establishment." Power's addictive pull was never so apparent and never so bipartisan in approach.

Voters are now witnessing leadership in its most undignified and cornered instincts.

Never before has this aspect been shared. Likewise, never again will promises trump performance.

Tea anyone?

Searches Violate Constitution

(November 28, 2010)

WHEN IS ENOUGH, ENOUGH? APPROXIMATELY a month before our Thanksgiving holidays, TSA has initiated new and personally intrusive security techniques which given the choice, is no choice.

One may either acquiesce to a revealing full body scanner/imaging or stand dutifully silent as a TSA agent manhandles all private body parts. One added feature is that in choosing the imaging, there is also a dose of radiation included.

There seems to be a purpose with commencing this program so close to the most heavily traveled of holidays. With family dinners hanging in the balance, this incentive may have value as an offset to stiff public reactions. After all, Washington has already proven its willingness to initiate policy irrespective of the public's wishes.

All this comes in response to the failed attempts from last year's Christmas Day bomber. As is usually the case, government's newest budding bureaucracy has issued a knee jerk overkill measure which not only misses its mark but also infuriates. Along with scheduled flights, the prospect of cancellations will also take off.

Amid this ongoing discourse, poignant opeds and public angst, one fundamental security issue remains ignored. We still have Fourth Amendment guarantees. To quote our Forefathers, in part, "The right of the people to be secure in their persons, houses, paper, and effects, against unreasonable searches and seizures shall not be violated, and no warrants shall issue, but upon probable cause . . ."

Prior to commencing searches upon public assemblages of peaceful and law abiding citizens, and due to the intimate nature of such searches, an expectation of citing "probable cause" must first be established. In fact, this entire need for ensuring "security" may be, in reality, an oxymoron in that the most precious of personal security has become the object for breeching.

Consider what is not examined. Experience gained from both prison searches and past drug smuggling operations have documented criminal usage of available body cavities. Neither the pat down nor the scanner address this possibility. Obviously, in terrorism speak, what is left unexamined will draw attention for possible success. So, what will be the next procedure in the name of security?

Aside from the cavity threat, consider the Muslim lady traveling in her Muslim garb. Which option could she choose? Would it be the undressing scanner or the hands on pat down? Since her only option is refusal, this entire safety charade becomes moot.

This Constitutional perversity conjures up memories when drunk drivers were menacing our highways. The most ominous effect created from the ensuing DUI legislations was the fishnet type of detection methods employed by police roadblocks. The law's creation necessitated a redirected target from "drunken" violators to violators exceeding a predetermined yet arbitrary Blood Alcohol Content (BAC) level. The crime became "under the influence" rather than citing a drunken condition.

Of immediate concern was then, as is now, our inalienable Fourth Amendment rights. The need for first establishing "probable cause" would either stand or fall. After weathering court challenges and initial public indignation, this legal obstacle was discarded for the preference of public safety. In retrospect, the cost for this legal abuse may be on the rise.

Concern for safety has once again resurfaced and is again becoming the clarion call against our Fourth Amendment. "Probable cause," in spite of past un-Constitutional court rulings, presents a legal deterrent to both the unreasonable highway searches and these demeaning and personally invasive airport screenings. The manner in which our Fourth Amendment rights were completely ignored, while creating this airport boondoggle, seems to be an outgrowth from the past precedence of DUI rulings. If this is allowed to go unanswered, what will differentiate our safety needs from scanners to cavity searches?

Security encompasses much more than abusing the rights of the individual. At what point is our Country's security equally as serious? How can we justify these "touchy feely" security pat downs when illegals of all sorts flood into our Country on a daily basis? The numbers are of such magnitude that it would be foolish to deny the existence of terrorists within any day's totals.

Is this airport security charade geared towards the safety of flying Americans or is it part of a continuing agenda aimed at reducing our Constitutional rights? These security loopholes and governmental overtures suggest the later.

Benjamin Franklin said it best. "They that give up essential liberty to obtain a little temporary safety deserve neither liberty or safety." Again, just how much is enough?

Living In Fear In The Land Of The Free

(December 20, 2010)

AMID THIS SEASON OF GIVING and thanks, a neighbor recently commented about a piece that I had written for the local paper. His questioning caused me to revisit my position and delve deeper into my original concerns.

Briefly, my essay questioned the reactive security measures that are now in place at various airports across our Country. My perspective centered upon our inalienable Fourth Amendment rights against unreasonable searches without probable cause. I likened this recent tactic to the now routine DUI roadblock investigations, which also lack probable cause.

My friend's contention was the "rode hard and hung up wet" reasoning that no search is too invasive if it will ensure safety in flight. He prefaced his remarks with the age old "our Forefathers had no ideas about air travel." I think the same alibi was recited about the "unknown" dangers from automobiles during the introductory period of DUI legislation.

With today's indiscriminate roadblock usage, we now are required, under the guilty penalty if choosing non compliance, to give "witness against himself" (herself) by breathe and/or blood. Again all for safety.

Returning to my neighbor, I agreed to his points that our Forefathers were ignorant as to future modes of transportation. However, my alarm centered upon the knee jerk acceptance to be safe, no matter the cost. At what point does this price become prohibitive? As is the case with too many today, he laughed off my objection as not being relevant with regards to the current terrorist threat. He had a point since who wants to die?

My neighbor, who I respect as a very confident and able bodied man sent me to wondering about this dilemma. Where is the middle ground?

Is there a middle ground? Is it part of this fast paced world or could it be a new slant on an age old nemesis?

My final reasoning found that yes, it was a problem which unfortunately has been common throughout the ages. In a very practical sense, it asks many questions and the answers test each and every American.

Elementary with freedom is its responsibilities. And are we willing to sacrifice in order to gain its rarefied station and preserve its blessings? If so, are we worthy?

As Americans, our blessings of freedom are inherent with our birth. We come to expect all that being an American has to offer. This may in fact be our weak link since what is given is never fully appreciated.

To live free incorporates a willingness to die for its preservation. That's what gives its credibility and strength. When valued, it cannot be defeated. What we are witnessing is the slow abandonment of its responsibilities and eventually, freedom's fire will be extinguished.

If there is no search too invasive, no insult too insulting, no groping too personal, then how do we expect to live free? What is the post "pat down" cost and how much is safety worth? What is left to ponder in our quiet but safe moments? What have we just permitted?

What it comes down to is that freedom isn't just a word, it's a belief, an inner strength, a resolve that cannot be taken away. It fortifies in similar fashion as does our religious intensities.

Our Forefathers actually valued freedom to the point that they were willing to die for its achievement. Their choice of life or death obviously didn't involve an airplane or an automobile but it did conjure up mental pictures of hanging at the end of a rope. They chose to live free and if need be die, but die as free men.

Compare those beginnings to our current society. We now shudder at any thought of insecurity. Think of our reaction when a passerby greets us or about thinking the worse of a hitchhiker. How many of us only feel secure in "gated communities?" We now are fearful of our children playing outside. We are even afraid to meet a stranger and instead opt for computer dating services.

Would it be fair to say that Americans today live in fear? They have magnified their own insecurities so that almost any feature of safety will be permitted. As such, this is no longer a free society. Today's passivity reflects a people who are connected with our Founders only by their American birth.

The answer to my neighbor is that talk is cheap, so is writing about it. Quoting Benjamin Franklin's "They that give up essential liberty to obtain a little temporary safety deserve neither liberty or safety" is to no avail. The reason? Because Americans today are afraid and the truth spouted by Franklin so long ago still rings fearfully true.

In the end, we all must die eventually. I realize that this is a very callous observation, one in which few wish to think about but nevertheless, it's true. I also understand that none of us wants to hurry up the process. But, in the living, it's how one lives that counts. Fear, or even tinges of fear that creep into decision making is not living free.

When Muslim women wearing Muslim attire are exonerated from pat downs and scanners, the entire façade of providing passenger/plane security is reduced to its very ugly state, which is nothing more than a "police" state. Is it any wonder why we already live in fear?

Victory For Constitution

(February 11, 2011)

THE MOST BLATANT ATTACK AGAINST our Constitution, last year's passage of Obama's health care legislation, met its match when U.S. District Court Judge Roger Vinson defended our Forefathers with his conclusion that, "If Congress can penalize a passive individual for failing to engage in commerce, the enumeration of powers in the Constitution would have been in vain." Finally, with those words, the constitution received the proper station for which its eminent legal status demands.

In recent years, our Constitution has endured a brazen public disregard and disdain from the very ones who have sworn to "preserve, protect and defend" its tenets. Take for instance an example from the 17th district in Illinois. Congressman Hare flagrantly epitomized his disrespect with this sad statement, "I don't care about the Constitution."

And we all are well aware of Rep. Pelosi's infamous "are you serious, are you serious" reply when asked if the proposed Healthcare package was Constitutional.

Well, contrary to Rep. Hare, there are millions of veterans who do care. I fully realize that there is a contingent of elected "public servants" who have a problem with its restrictive message. However, their attempts to weasel and squirm from its dictates only adds validation to our Forefathers concerns and for their emphasis upon governmental restraints.

We all should find it a bit overbearing that in view of this recent legal finding, the Obama Administration intends to "proceed to carry out the law."

Administration spokesmen critiqued the Judge's decision as "a plain case of judicial overreaching."

In posting this arrogant position to the public, it confirms two unavoidable conclusions. One, they lack any respect for the average

American's Constitutional understanding. Secondly, they intend to conduct our government in a lawless fashion. As such, it now becomes impossible to ignore their despotic manners and intentions.

Brought about by their numerical superiority in Congress, the democrats went about coercing, buying and intimidating the necessary votes required for the bill's passage. This was carried out with full and complete appreciation that it would eventually victimize our Constitution's most sacred blessing—individual liberty and freedom.

This fact can hardly be overlooked or easily dismissed. There is not one Constitutional fiber which could remotely legitimize its socialistic essence. Yet, elected public servants defiled their oaths of office in voting for its passage.

The Obama Administration has tied its Health Care bill to the ever—expanding "commerce clause" defined in Article I, Section 8, Clause 3 of our Constitution. It briefly states, under the list of powers assigned, that Congress has the power "To regulate commerce with foreign nations, and among the several States, and with the Indian tribes."

Seems to be a normal consideration when creating a unifying government from so many sovereign and independent States. However, the original normalcy associated with interstate commerce has been greatly inflated over time to include wetlands regulations, authority over who must be served in restaurants, controls over wages and product prices and of what and the amount to which a farmer may grow. It even goes so far as to employ this clause against one who refuses to deal on an interstate basis since it affects the balance of commerce from a negative aspect.

Amid my later years, I have witnessed a growing social bias against American ideals. Everything traditional is now passé or worse.

I also see a growing sentiment for the appetite of "something for nothing." This has been the subliminal message infused into our lottery fascinations. Now, it's morphed over to health care. Of course, when our economy dumps, these "something for nothing" expectations soar.

The well worn adage, nothing is free, has withstood any and all slick promotions. Obviously, covering an additional thirty million uninsured will be an additional and unavoidable cost.

Also in the mix, consider just what the federal government has ever accomplished efficiently? Since the answer is "nothing," why would sane citizens even consider giving authority for their health maintenance to such a bumbling entity? Have we all been caught up into this expectation of "something for nothing?" If so, gambling on our physical welfare may well be the finale to losing our mental acumen.

In conclusion, governments always seek additional authority. Good intentions are its façade. So, and as it should be, it will always be up to us to maintain not only our own health but also our Constitution. In the end, our interest in both should be unquestionably keener than that of some distant bureaucrat. The timing to Judge Vinson's decision accomplished both.

Dysfunctional Government Problems Mount

(March 28, 2011)

OUR AMERICAN GOVERNMENT HAS BECOME a fuzz ball for dysfunctional activity. Consider our mounting debt, quickly while it still hovers around fourteen trillion.

Check out all the State governments, especially the ones most privy to ongoing border invasions, which Washington refuses to even address. And how about the ease of initiating combat operations since the scuttling of the draft? Today, it appears to be Libya's turn in the democracy barrel. Last, but far from the least is our ongoing Constitutional crisis which our media generally chooses to ignore.

Can anyone get past the politics of politics for a minute in order to judge the inept insanity of our budget quagmire? Last year's democratically controlled Congress refused their basic responsibility for addressing the following year's budget. Reason tells us that few wanted their names associated with the coming fall elections. So, if this becomes the norm, every other year will feature Congress passing the previous and the next year's budget. As such, we the people may enjoy a reprieve from additional legislation during the year taken up by financial bickering.

Contrast Washington with the governmental leadership in Wisconsin. Here is a Governor, who recognizes the mounting injury to his State and its citizens yet suffers every abuse printable from our media. Given that Wisconsin is not a border State, the red ink still signals the need for change.

Also, I fail to see the need or reason for college students to act like spoiled little children while their contribution to the work force is still in waiting.

As a survivor from enforcing Washington's foreign melees, I shudder when thinking of the unremitting overseas deployments which our "volunteer army" is asked to endure, all without Congressional backup. As the saying goes, "some things never change." It certainly bears consideration as to the free hand which this volunteer service has presented to bureaucratic bravehearts. Other than Lt. Calley, just who is accountable for our losses?

If all this isn't bad enough, we at home have been fettered under an ongoing constitutional defiance that somehow does not merit journalistic attention.

In recounting this gross injustice to the enumerated powers of government, back room deals, bribery and collusion greased the Congressional passage of a health care bill which the average "man in the street" readily understands to be unconstitutional. Still, Congressional passage led to the bill's presidential signing.

State after State joined in legal action against this usurpation into our medical industry. As it stands, after a Florida District Court of the United States ruled the entire health care law unconstitutional, the Obama administration continued on without any pause or recognition to the court order.

Having his ruling defiled, Judge Vinson once again ordered the defendants, in this case, the U.S. Department of Health and Human Services, to file an appeal "within seven calendar days." This appeal, which was filed just within the specified time, is merely a formality prior to a Supreme Court review. As mentioned, anyone with a working familiarity of our Constitution fully acknowledges the law's unconstitutionality. And sadly, this is just one instance of this Administration's flagrant defiance.

For too long, the state of Arizona has been victimized by years of illegal entry from foreigners. As one of our Southwestern States, Arizona has endured what our Constitution aptly terms an "invasion." This disorder has reached the levels of outright criminal activity which has caused brutal loss of American lives.

Article IV, Section 4 of our Constitution plainly states, "The United States shall guarantee to every State in this Union a republican form of government, and shall protect each of them against invasion . . ." Not only has this protection been adamantly refused to Arizona, the Federal Government has taken legal steps against that State. Washington has also joined in a different lawsuit against Arizona with other foreign countries.

The time is long since past when political ideologies carried the day. We are all Americans and what is done to one is done to all. I find it terrifying that this abandonment of one of our States can take place without a public outcry. This Constitutional safeguard is exactly the meat of our NATO alliance of mutual assurance.

Should Arizona or our law of the land be of lesser importance? As this crisis continues, our media still finds difficulty in severing its umbilical cord with Obama. This dysfunctional behavior is classic to that of an enabler.

Facts Don't Lie: U.S. Is Inept

(July 9, 2011)

CALL ME OUT OF SYNC, Neanderthal or just your run of the mill extremist but facts do not lie. Never before has America been so inept at everything. Such consistency alludes to an agenda not yet revealed.

This hidden abstract is past the giddiness and flim-flam notoriety which so often springs from the infamous "conspiracy" windmills. No sir, we are at a crossroads in the American experiment which may well evolve into a dead end. During the last fifty some years, traditions, standards, even normal thinking has drastically been refined, and in many cases, reversed. This social/economic/governmental engineering has marginalized common sense and as per the governmental spectrum, has defied long standing laws which previously had been enforced and publicly accepted.

The list is as long as it is varied. Pick an area or a current dilemma and then recount its transitions during the last fifty years. I don't care what the subject matter is, the change has produced either counter productive or negative results.

First to consider is the democrat's paragon of Presidential excellence, FDR. If I may, one of his lesser known quotes is the warning that, "In politics, nothing happens by accident. If it happens, you can bet it was planned that way." This may serve as our discussion format since much of what has transpired has often been blamed upon bad decision-making or unfortunate happenstance. But again, this enduring consistency makes such a possibility highly unlikely; that is if the law of probability still matters.

My particular age permits me to connect many forgotten historical dots. One is Nikita Khrushchev's 1962 declaration that, "the United States will eventually fly the communist Red Flag . . ." That was forty-nine years ago.

Another seldom mentioned fact is that in the year in which I was born, 1944, there existed only one communist country, the USSR. So, despite our efforts and sacrifice in places such as Korea and Vietnam, that "red flag" is continuing to rise.

Our Country began with a previously unheard of formula. Our Declaration of Independence explicitly detailed that, "we hold these truths to be self evident, that all men are created equal; that they are endowed by their Creator with certain unalienable rights . . ." I cite this new beginning in order to correlate our current withering allegiance with freedom verses the consistent spread of that "red flag."

I lived during an era when China was our sworn enemy and remember its former identity as Red China. I also remember prayer in school, patriotic singing and societal restrictions due to Sunday being a day of Christian worship.

I often wondered as to the need for our creation of the United Nations when at the time, we were the only nuclear power. This folly was then magnified as America joined what has from its first day had socialistic and/or communist leadership.

On the home front, I remember when authority was our society's glue. When the parent took the word from another adult verses the protests of innocence from their children. And of course, the innocence with a bag of marbles or the commonness of the penknife taken to school.

There was a day when our heroes wore white hats and rode a white horse. In fact, our daily genre of "cowboys and Indians" were without the current short comings of addiction. To catch a glimpse of these differing "good guy" portrayals, check the original John Wayne "True Grit" with the current version. The roughly five minutes it took Rooster to get out of bed is typical of today's reluctant and dysfunctional hero.

There is a public freak show on a daily parade which more than validates this growing lack of societal authority and order. Our current crop of 'lil darlings' rule the family roast. Modern day parents deem being buddies over being disciplinarians. And the results are sadly evident.

Our government and our sliding economy attests to what happens when good intentions and limitless authority becomes the norm. Corruption, which was formerly relegated to Washington has now spread throughout our countryside in the forms of hand outs and subsidized grants. Our federal authority now commands our submission at both a State and individual level. For our own good, we are being instructed in our most rudimentary of daily needs by big brother. Light bulbs, toilet flushes, even permission for back yard digging all come under the purview of governmental care.

Those of us who can make the distinction from then till now are becoming more active and informed. This reaction is not political, it springs from the instinct for self preservation. While our economy takes the headlines, America has been subjected to this transitional period which will not strengthen or even permit her experiment in freedom to endure.

How we react will determine our future. Hard decisions and difficult challenges lie ahead. Our generation is being called upon, as others have been. And in sync with our predecessors, the ideals which America represents are still worthy of our devotion and undying loyalty.